12 STEPS TO TRUE LOVE & LONG-LASTING PEACE AND INTIMACY

EVERY SPOUSE NEEDS TO KNOW

DR. MALICK KOUYATE

BALBOA.PRESS
A DIVISION OF HAY HOUSE

Balboa Press books may be ordered through booksellers or by contacting:

Balboa Press
A Division of Hay House
1663 Liberty Drive
Bloomington, IN 47403
www.balboapress.com
844-682-1282

Print information available on the last page.

ISBN: 978-1-9822-6650-9 (sc)
ISBN: 978-1-9822-6651-6 (hc)
ISBN: 978-1-9822-6652-3 (e)

Library of Congress Control Number: 2021906686

Balboa Press rev. date: 04/07/2021

CONTENTS

PART IV

How to Share the 3 Types of true Love and Long Lasting Peace and Intimacy every Would be an Excellent Spouse Needs to Know?

TO THE READERS

Dear readers, eighteenth-century French philosopher, Francois-Marie Arouet, commonly known as Voltaire, said:

There are two ways of dying:
★disappearing physically, that's natural and nothing,
★but loving and being not loved, that's unbearable.

Many spouses from many social and cultural backgrounds of so many different corners of the world are dying alive. They still love but they are no longer loved.

There are many spouses who do not know how to love with true *Love.*

There are many other spouses who do not know how to be loved with true *Love.*

There are many spouses who do not enjoy and share true *Love, Peace* and *Intimacy* with each other.

Yet, true *Love* and long-lasting *Peace* and *Intimacy* in marriage are some of the world's most intense and most sought after socially inspired human passions.

But, true *Love* and long-lasting *Peace* and *Intimacy* in marriage are also some of the world's most difficult to find, enjoy and share human passions.

True *Love* and long-lasting *Peace* and *Intimacy* in marriage require inner purity, maturity, self-control, inner peace, forgiveness, healing, wholeness, a meaningful life, a fulfilled life, compassion...which all may involve but encompass by far name, fame, power position, material possessions...

But, as goes the old saying:

No one marries their true fiance.

Indeed, before or soon after the wedding ceremonies, many spouses from many different walks of life may start wondering where is the wonderful fiance they fell in love with?

Before or soon after the wedding ceremonies, spouses start unmasking their *Persona-mask.* They start unveiling parts of their true and total *Personality*, including:

- ★ *the dark and ugly side of their Personal Unconscious,*
- ★ *the rejected and repressed side of their Personal Unconscious,*
- ★ *the stubborn and difficult to control side of their Personal Unconscious.*

Yesterday's wonderful fiance is slowly but steadily becoming today's unpredictable *spouse with no hope for true Love and long-lasting Peace and Intimacy with each other.*

Men blame women for the lack of *Love, Peace* and *Intimacy* in their marriage.

Women blame men for the lack of *Love, Peace* and *Intimacy* in their marriage.

Who is right?

Who is wrong?

Can both men and women be both right and wrong at the same time? No one seems to know for sure. What is sure is that the lack of true *Love, Peace* and *Intimacy* in marriage is dragging many spouses of all walks of life into the bottomless abyss of nothingness or what neurologist and logo-therapist Viktor E. Frankl calls:

- ★ *existential vacuum,*
- ★ *existential frustration,*
- ★ *the frustrated will to pleasure at its lowest level.*

Why so many headaches, heartbreaks and tears on the long, rocky and slippery road to:

- ★ *true and long-lasting Love in marriage?*
- ★ *true and long-lasting Peace in marriage?*
- ★ *true and long-lasting Intimacy in marriage?*

Dear spouses,
The first and the most costly marriage's mistakes
is to fall in love with and get married to each other's
natural and normal but too often too superficial
Persona-mask instead of each other's
true and total Personality.

Marriage's necessity for closeness, consistency and intimacy pushes spouses to unmask their *Persona-mask*. Marriage, more than anything else, is a place where there is nowhere to hide.

In marriage, spouses unveil parts of their true and total *Personality*, including *the dark, ugly, stubborn and so difficult to control side of their Personal Unconscious.*

Depth psychologist, Carl G. Jung, characterizes the *Personal Unconscious* as the parts of our personality incompatible with our social norms...

For example, a controlling spouse sees his/her way as the only way. It's all about his/her:

- ★ *I, me, mine, myself...*
- ★ *my way or no other way...*
- ★ *self-aggrandizement, domineering and demeaning attitudes...*

But, in life, in love and in marriage:

- ★ *the common ground is the ideal playground,*
- ★ *the win-win is marriage's happiness winning style,*
- ★ *the middle is marriage's ideal pathway to stability.*

Dear spouses, do you want to know how to:

- ★ love each other with true and long-lasting *Love*?
- ★ enjoy and share true and long-lasting *Peace and Intimacy*?
- ★ be *One* with one another without losing your personal *Identity*?

If *Yes* is your answer, you then need also to know why and how to enjoy and share:

- ★ *the healthy and free and fully alive innocent Inner Child within both of you,*
- ★ *true and long-lasting Fulfillment for both of you,*
- ★ *true and long-lasting Inner Peace so vital to your Peace and Intimacy.*

Excellent marriage hinges on *Excellence* in education or your *Oneness with full Self-awareness with:*

- ★ *your own true, transcendent, infinite Self,*
- ★ *each other's true Self,*
- ★ *everyone else's true Self.*

Excellence in *education* is the *Panacea* or universal remedy against:

- ★ *the Fear of Life or the Fear of Death or the Empty Center,*
- ★ *marriage's instabilitirs, infidelities and bitter divorce,*
- ★ *all man-made tragedies.*

But your *Excellence* in education has little or nothing to do with your high academic achievements, your deep knowledge, your vast practical skills, your extraordinary success...

Your *Excellence* in education has everything to do with your will, skills and wisdom to know why and how to act, interact and react, ideally at the same time, as:

- ★ *social human beings,*
- ★ *individual human beings,*
- ★ *spiritual beings.*

You both are meant to know why and how to enjoy and share the *Powerful* life animating *Power* of the *Balance* and the *Harmony* between your:

- ★ *life's inevitable Conflicts,*
- ★ *personal inner Opposites,*
- ★ *Persona-mask and your true and total Personality.*

To know how to enjoy and share true *Love* and long-lasting *Peace* and *Intimacy* with each other, you must know why and how to:

- ★ *be in Love with your own true Self first if you are to be in Love with each other,*
- ★ *be in Peace with your own true Self first if you are to be in Peace with each other,*
- ★ *be Intimate with your own true Self first if you are to be Intimate with each other.*

Ancient Greek philosopher, Plato, said:

Everyone sings a song, incomplete
until another heart whispers back.
Those who wish to sing always find a song.
At the touch of a lover, everyone becomes a poet.

Excellent spouses, like great poets, know why and how to:

- ★ *read each other between the lines,*
- ★ *see in each other more than eye can see,*
- ★ *enjoy and share each other's deep needs.*

To share true *Love*, *Peace* and *Intimacy*, you need to know why and how to:

- ★ *be in touch with the best there is deep within and all around both of you,*
- ★ *be deeply touched by the best there is deep within and all around both of you,*
- ★ *tap into the Magic between the best there is deep within and all around both of you.*

YOU & ME

Dear spouse,
Let the *You* in *Me* and the *Me in You*
Meet and meltdown and be *One,*
One with one another without losing
Our *Personal Identity.*
When we lose, for any reason,
Our *Personal Identity,*
We have nothing worthy left in our *Inner Life.*

Let the *You* in *Me* and the *Me* in *You*
Be the *source,* the *essence,* the *quintessence,*
The *heart, the soul and the spirit*
Of the *Us* in *You* and the *Us* in *Me.*
Let *healthy self-love, let spiritual love,*
Let unconditional love
Be the smoothest and the straightest road
Between the best there is within *You*
and all around *You,*
And the best there is within *Me*
and all around *Me.*

Let enjoy and share and celebrate
The will, the skills and the wisdom
We need to know *why* and *how*
To love each other with:
**true and long-lasting Love,*
**true and long-lasting Peace,*
**true and long-lasting Intimacy.*

MEET DR. MALICK KOUYATE

Thank you so much for trusting me with your time, energy and resources.

My name is Malick Kouyate. I am from Guinea, Conakry, West Africa.

I am the author of *How To Educate All For Excellence (Trafford Publishing, 2013)* and *All For Excellence In Education: 9 Steps To Every Child's Inner Splendor (Balboa Press, 2020) and the co-founder of ALL FOR EXCELLENCE IN EDUCATION (AFEIE)*.

Early on in my life, my parents, like all loving parents, used to tell me that:

- ★ *God, because of His omnipotence and a baby, because of his innocence, deal both with the heart. Therefore, if I smile at a baby who refuses to smile back, mine is not from my heart.*
- ★ *a child is a love letter written by a whole family at the service of the whole community. Therefore, every step I take and move I make and action I undertake, I must do so with my whole family and my whole community in my heart.*
- ★ *if the whole world stands on this side, stand still on your own side as long as you know that you are right from the bottom of your own heart. Therefore, I must be true to my own true Self at any cost even at the cost of being cast out.*

Some of the steps I took and moves I made and the actions I undertook did not meet my parents' expectations.

I have had my own lion share of missteps, mistakes, fears, failures, lacks and temporary setbacks.

But, what my parents taught me is still ringing, like a bygone musical melody, into the back of my mind.

Looking back, I realize that my parents wanted me to know why and how to act, interact and react, ideally at the same time, as:

- ★ *a social human being,*
- ★ *a personal human being,*
- ★ *a spiritual being.*

Unfortunately, I left my parents when I was only 16 years old. Upon their agreement, I went away to pursue my schooling.

In sharp contrast to *the time tested ways of life, shared values and solid worldviews* my parents wanted me to live by, some of my new life exposures and experiences away from my parents were implicitly telling me that:

- ★ *whom I know is more important than what I know,*
- ★ *what I have is more important than who I am,*
- ★ *name, fame, and fortune are more important than shared values,*
- ★ *why then should I bother?*

On the one hand, I love my parents with all my heart. I believe, almost religiously, in all what they taught me.

To try to defy or deny what they told me was to try to defy or deny a vital part of me. To me, that was impossible.

On the other hand, a great deal of what was going on all around me, once away from my parents' home was too obvious to be denied too.

As a French phenomenologist philosopher,
Merleau Ponty said:

No one can deny evidence,
you have to follow it
or to flee from it.

I was confused. I did not know what to say. I did not know what to do. I did not know which way to go. I was in limbo.

Have you ever been too confused too?

What I love the most...*my integrity and inner autonomy*...collided with what I hate the most...*hypocrisy and blind conformity.*

My innocent *Inner Child* was deeply wounded,
My *Inner Void* was deep and unfathomable,
My *Inner Voice* was temporally silenced,
The pain of my *Inner Emptiness*
Was ineffable and unbearable.
What do you do when
It is so little or nothing else left to do?

It is in the midst of such *a do-or-die situation* that I started listening more regularly and more attentively to my own small and still *Inner Voice.*

My *Inner Voice* was telling me to hold on tight. My *Inner Voice* was telling me to rely on, learn from and build upon the ineffable *something more and bigger and better deep* within me and all around me.

Call it divine love, divine grace, divine guidance... Call it healthy self-love, spiritual love, unconditional love... The *Larger* than *Life* deep within me and all around me has been my first and one of the most *Vital Life-Saving Signals* on my long and often rocky and slippery road to *Excellence In Education.*

I realize that true and unconditional *Love* is my smoothest and straightest road to the ineffable place, deep within me and all around me, where I am divinely, spiritually, and psychologically meant to:

- ⋆ *love truly, live fully alive, forgive, forget, heal, be whole...*
- ⋆ *see all men as the same important members of the same family: the Human Family...*

- ★ *be a peaceful culture consumer and become a mindful culture producer...*

But true love cannot be taught,
True love cannot be bought,
True love can only be caught,
For true love to be caught,
True love must be part
Of all we do,
True love must be part
Of all we refuse to do.

However, it took me over 48 years to understand why and how to enjoy and share:

- ★ *the powerful life-giving and animating power of true Love,*
- ★ *the powerful life-giving and animating power of the Larger than Life,*
- ★ *the powerful life-giving and animating power deep within me and around me.*

From now on till the day I die, my mission in life is to inspire all age-appropriate interested children in general and all open-minded interested teens, adolescents and young adults, in particular, to know *why* and *how* to build a two-way learning road between their too often conflicting:

- ★ *two children in every child,*
- ★ *two learning worlds in every teaching-learning environment,*
- ★ *two learning outcomes in every teaching-learning process.*

Dear spouses, within a few months or weeks or days or even hours, I will, if I have the opportunity, inspire all interested would be *Excellent* spouses to know *why* and *how* to:

- ★ *love truly, live fully alive, forgive, forget, heal, be whole...*
- ★ *love their own self with healthy self-love,*
- ★ *love each other with true Love and long-lasting Peace and Intimacy.*

DEDICATION

This book is dedicated to my wife, the love of my life.
You teach me, without a single word, how to love truly
You teach me how to live fully alive,
You teach me how to forgive, forget, heal, be whole,
You teach me how to enjoy and share...
A meaningful and peaceful life
In a meaningful and peaceful world...
Meaning and peace so vital
To my openness and receptivity
To *Ultimate Meaning* or *Super-Meaning*.

This book is also dedicated to all open-minded
Would be loving spouses
Of all walks of life who all want to know why and how to:
★*love their own self with healthy Self-love,*
★*love each other with true and long-lasting Love,*
★*enjoy and share true and long-lasting Peace and Intimacy with each other.*

The 12 *Vital* but too often missing *Life Saving Signals*
On your long and too often rocky and slippery road
To true *Love* and long-lasting *Peace* and *Intimacy*
With each other are:
★*the healthy and free and fully alive innocent*
Inner Child within both of you,
★*the true and long-lasting Fulfillment for both of you,*
★*the true and long-lasting Inner Peace for both of you,*
★*meaningfulness,*
★*mindfulness,*
★*the more than eye can see within both of you,*
★*the more than Need-love for both of you,*
★*the more than Gift-love for both of you,*

★the more than Mature-love for both of you,
★healthy self-love,
★spiritual love,
★unconditional love.

ACKNOWLEDGEMENTS

A book on *True Love and long-lasting Peace and Intimacy Every Loving Spouse Needs To Know* is an inspiration of the world's great:

- ★ *religious and spiritual traditions,*
- ★ *collective wisdom,*
- ★ *solid worldviews.*

The world great religious and spiritual traditions and collective wisdom tell us that:

- ★ *we each and all are created at God-image,*
- ★ *we each and all are created at God-likeness,*
- ★ *God is all-loving, all-knowing, all-powerful...*

For all true believers, that means that we each and all are divinely/ spiritually meant to be:

- ★ *all-loving,*
- ★ *all-knowing,*
- ★ *all-powerful.*

But, our day-to-day life inevitable *Conflicts*, our natural and normal pairs of personal inner *Opposites,* our hurtful friends and foes, and our possible fears, failures, lacks, and temporary setbacks are also telling us that we each and all are merely:

- ★ *what we know,*
- ★ *what we do,*
- ★ *what we have.*

Dear spouses, the larger the gap between who we are divinely/ spiritually meant to be and whom we happen to be in our day-to-day life, the deeper the wound we may inflict on anyone close to us including the very innocent *Inner Child* deep within every one of us.

Dear spouses,
You cannot enjoy and share true *Love* and
long-lasting *Peace and Intimacy*
With each other when one or both of you face the faceless face
Of what neurologist and psychiatrist and logo-therapist,
Viktor Emil Frankl, calls:
★*existential vacuum,*
★*existential frustration.*
★*the frustrated will to meaning, to power, to money, and to pleasure.*

I am so grateful and thankful to all those who inspire me to know why and how to:

- ★ *be in touch with the Larger than Life deep within me,*
- ★ *be deeply touched by the Larger than Life all around me,*
- ★ *tap into the magic between the best there is within me and all around me.*

INTRODUCTION

Their own Words

Pitirim Sorokin, author of
The Ways and Power of Love, said:

Love is like an iceberg: only a small part of it
is visible and even the visible part is little known...
Love appears to be a universe inexhaustible
qualitatively and quantitatively.

Dear spouses, *Repetition, Repetition, Repetition*, that's a smooth road to:

- ★ *active learning,*
- ★ *meaningful learning,*
- ★ *mindful learning.*

Repetition, Repetition, Repetition, that's a fast road to:

- ★ *the common ground, your marriage's ideal playground,*
- ★ *the win-win, your marriage's happiness winning style,*
- ★ *the middle, your marriage's ideal pathway to wisdom.*

Dear spouses, the Fulani of Futa Djallo, Guinea, West Africa,
have an old saying that goes:

If your friend is richer than you, be a good shepherd,
If your friend is more knowledgeable than you, be very good at social skills,
If your friend's mother is better than your mother, have a better wife,
If your friend's wife is better than yours, stop the fight, follow him and eat.

People of all walks of life have inspiring ideas about the role and importance of a stable and happy marriage.

True *Love* and long-lasting *Peace* and *Intimacy* in a marriage are some of the most intense human passions.

But, true *Love* and long-lasting *Peace and Intimacy* in a marriage are also some of the most difficult human passions to find and to enjoy, and share.

Dear spouses, if you are to know how to enjoy and share true *Love* and long-lasting *Peace* and *Intimacy* with each other, you need to know first how to enjoy and share true *Love* and long-lasting *Peace and Intimacy* with your own true *Self.*

You are your own first best friend.

You may be your own worst enemy.

The choice is all yours.

Choose wisely. Choose to be your own first best friend.

When one or both of you face the faceless face of your *wounded* innocent *Inner Child*, your deep and unfathomable *Inner Void* and your ineffable and unbearable *Pain of Inner Emptiness*, you may not know why and how to:

- ★ *enjoy healthy self-love,*
- ★ *share healthy self-love,*
- ★ *celebrate true Love and long-lasting Peace and Intimacy with each other.*

Your true *Love* for each other and your long-lasting *Peace* and *Intimacy* with each other hinge upon:

- ★ *the healthy and free and fully alive innocent Inner Child within both of you,*
- ★ *the true and long-lasting Fulfillment for both of you,*
- ★ *the Harmony between the natural pairs of your personal inner Opposites, such as your:*

1. *Consciousness and Unconscious,*
2. *Ego and Shadow,*
3. *Persona-mask and true Personality.*

True *Love* and long-lasting *Peace and Intimacy* with each other requires your will, skills, and wisdom to:

- ⋆ *love truly, live fully alive, forgive, forget, heal, be whole...*
- ⋆ *enjoy and share a meaningful, peaceful life, purposeful life...*
- ⋆ *welcome the emergence of each other's true, transcendent, infinite Self.*

Your happy or unhappy marriage may teach you life-changing lessons.

Ancient Greek philosopher, Socrates, said:

Marry in all means.
If you find a good wife,
you will be happy.
If you find a bad one,
you will be a philosopher.

Once you know why and how to enjoy and share true *Love* and long-lasting *Peace and Intimacy* with each other, you will be some of the world's happiest people alive.

Their Own Story

There is a Chinese popular story of "The Butterfly Lovers."
This popular Love story dates back to the Tang Dynasty (618-907).

This Love story is about a woman named
Zhu Yingtai. She disguises herself
as a man in order to pursue her studies in a distant city. In this distant city,
she met a male fellow student named Liang Shambo.
They became best friends.

When Zhu Yingtai was ordered by her parents to return home, she invited
her best friend to visit her so that she would
introduce him to her younger sister.
Her best friend discovered Zhu Yingtai's true identity as a young woman.

They fell in love with each other and woe eternal true Love for one another.
But the wealthy parents of the woman, Zhu Yingtai, have already given her
in marriage to another man.

Forced apart, Liang Shambo went back home to die of a broken heart.

Zhu Yingtai learns of her best friend's death during her wedding day.

She too dies the same day.

Her tears move heaven and earth. The ground cracks open.
She leaps to die beside the true Love of her life.

Today, the two true lovers are transformed into two beautiful butterflies flying together near each other forever.

Dear spouses, when one or both of you do not know how to love with true *Love* and long-lasting *Peace* and *Intimacy,* you may experience a stressful marriage.

A stressful marriage may affect your:

- ★ *immune system, mental stability, emotional balance...*
- ★ *lofty purpose, your worthy cause, your productivity...*
- ★ *trustworthiness, spontaneity, joyfulness, happiness, intimacy...*

In their own Words

In their book, *The Art Of Marriage Maintenance,*
Sylvia R. Karusa, MD and T. Ryam Karusa, MD,
reported the nightmare of a stressed-out husband.

"I don't know what I am going to find when I get home.
One day she is sweet and loving, calls me at the office, and tells me
how much she loves me, that I am the kindest
and the most generous of all men...

"Another day, she is angry, if not hostile,
screams at me at the top of her voice
that she hates me, that she hates me all her life but now more so,
because I am inconsiderate, rude, and the stingiest man she ever met...

"In either situation, I never know what I have done
to deserve the praise or the damnation..."

Dear spouses,
the first biggest and most costly marriage's mistake
is to fall in love with and marry each other's
mere Persona-mask at the detriment
of each other's true and total Personality.

Depth psychologist, Carl G. Jung, characterizes the *Persona-mask* as simple:

- ⋆ *masquerade,*
- ⋆ *or facade,*
- ⋆ *or social wrapping.*

When you deal with each other's true and total *Personality,* it will be easier for both of you to say when you have to:

- ⋆ *it is my fault,*
- ⋆ *I am so sorry,*
- ⋆ *please, forgive me.*

As human beings, we each and all are, to some degree, feeble, vulnerable, and fallible. We each and all may make mistakes.

Yet, as French old saying goes:

A truly confessed mistake is already half forgiven.

To hide behind your simple *Persona-mask* makes you small.

To deal with your true and total *Personality* makes you great.

American writer, Mark Twain, said:

Stay away from people who belittle you.
Small people always belittle you.
Great people make you feel great.

Dear spouses,

The purpose of this book is to make you feel great
Anytime, anywhere and under almost
Any life circumstances
When you are fighting with all your might
To know why and how to:

★*balance your life's inevitable Conflicts,*
★*harmonize your personal inner Opposites,*
★*accept, respect, and protect each others' innocent Inner Child,*
★*enjoy and share each other's true and long-lasting Fulfillment,*
★*enjoy and share Inner Peace so vital to your Peace with each other,*
★*accept and respect and tolerate your natural difference,*
★*awaken the positive side of each other's Sleeping Giant that is in no other,*
★*treasure each other's Priceless Inner Treasure that is in no other,*
★*share each other's life most favorite Love Song*
that has never been sung before,
★*celebrate true Love and long-lasting Peace and Intimacy with one another.*

Their own Words

In talking about modern *Marriage,* psychologist, Carl Rogers, said:

Though modern Marriage is a tremendous laboratory,
its members are often...without preparation
for the partnership function. How much agony and remorse
and failure could have been avoided if had there been
at least some rudimentary learning before
they entered the partnership.

Love Is The Road

Dear loving spouses,
Healthy self-love, spiritual love, unconditional love
Is
Your smoothest and straightest and fastest road to:
★true and long-lasting Inner Peace,
★true and long-lasting Peace with each other,
★true and long-lasting Intimacy with each other.

Healthy self-love, spiritual love, unconditional love
Is
Your smoothest and straightest and fastest road
To the powerful life-giving and life-animating power
Of the *Balance and Harmony* between your:
★life natural and normal and inevitable Conflicts,
★life natural and normal pairs of personal inner Opposites,
★personal Inclination and your loved ones' Expectations.

True love for your own true *Self,*
True love for each other's true *Self,*
True love for all, including your worst enemies' true *Self*
Is
Your best road to:
★the positive side of the Sleeping Giant within you that is in no other,
★the Priceless Inner Treasure in you that is in no other,
★the most favorite Love Song in you that has never been sung before.

PART I

How to Face the Parenting 3 Massive Mistakes that Prevent Would be Loving Spouses from Knowing Why and How To Love their own Self with Healthy Self-love?

The greatest way to live
with honor in this world
is to be
what we pretend to be.
(Socrates, philosopher)

Dear spouses,

The parenting 3 massive mistakes
That prevent would be loving spouses
From knowing why and how to:
★love their own self with Healthy Self-love,
★love each other with true and long-lasting Love,
★enjoy and share true and long-lasting Peace and Intimacy
are:
What psychologist of *Artistic Creativity*, Otto Rank,
And depth psychologist, Carl G. Jung, call:
★the Fear of Life (Otto Rank),
★the Fear of Death (Otto Rank),
★the Empty Center (Carl G. Jung).

Healthy self-love,
Spiritual love for each other and for all,
Unconditional love for each other and for all
Including your hurtful friends and foes,
are:
What you need first
If you are to know why and how to:
★prevent successfully,
★or confront constructively,
★and overcome definitively:
★the Fear of Life,
★the Fear of Death,
★the Empty Center.

CHAPTER 1

Heal The Inner Child

Step 1

Dear spouses, ***Step 1*** *to true Love and long-lasting Peace*
and Intimacy every loving spouse needs to know is the Powerful
life-giving and life animating Power of the Healthy and Free
and fully Alive innocent Inner Child deep within both of you.

Dear spouses,
The parenting first massive mistake
Or parents and important others' way as almost the only way
Or what the psychologist of *Artistic Creativity,*
Otto Rank, calls the *Fear of Life*
May limit certain teens, adolescents, and young adults
To blind conformity to their external authorities
At the detriment of their own *self-identity* and *inner anatomy.*

Parents and important others' way as almost the only way
May limit certain children to mere participation mystique.
Parents with their own wounded innocent *Inner Child*
May wound everyone else's innocent Inner Child,
Including their own children's innocent *Inner Child.*

Married couples who have been victims of the *Fear of Life*
May not know why and how to navigate smoothly
Between their first deepest need for *Belonging*
And their second deepest and equally important
Need for relative *Independence.*
The *Imbalance* between the two first deepest
And equally important educational needs

Is the first and one of the worst root causes of;

★*all educational failures at all levels,*

★*all domestic violence…*

★*all man-made tragedies...*

Their own Words

Mystic poet, Jalal U. Rumi, said:

Your task is not to seek love,
but merely seek…
all the barriers within yourself…
against it.

Dear spouses,
The first *Vital* but too often missing *Life Saving Signal*
On the long road to true *Love* and long-lasting *Peace* and *Intimacy*
Every would-be loving spouse needs to know
Is
The healthy and free and fully alive innocent
INNER CHILD
Deep within both spouses.

You cannot enjoy and share true and long-lasting:
**healthy self-love,*
**love for each other,*
**peace and intimacy with each other*
When one or both of you face the faceless face
Of a disowned and wounded innocent
INNER CHILD
Deep within one or both of you.

The first *Vital* but too often missing *Life Saving Signal*
On the long road to true *Love* and long-lasting *Peace* and *Intimacy*
You need to know
Is
Your ever-increasing and never-ending striving

To know why and how to accept and respect and protect
The healthy and free and fully alive innocent
INNER CHILD
Deep within both of you.

Dear spouses,
The best would be loving spouses among you
May not know why and how
To enjoy and share true and long-lasting:
★healthy self-love,
★love for each other,
★peace and intimacy with each other
When one or both of you face the faceless face
Of the wounded and marginalized innocent
INNER CHILD
Deep with one or both of you.

If you are to enjoy and share true and long-lasting:
★healthy self-love,
★love for each other,
★peace and intimacy with each other,
You need to know why and how to:
★accept and respect and protect your own innocent Inner Child,
★accept and respect and protect each other's innocent Inner Child,
★enjoy and share and celebrate each other's innocent Inner Child.

The healthy and free and fully alive innocent *Inner Child*
Deep within both of you has little or nothing to do
With your longing for celebrity and popularity
Or your name, fame, fortune, power position,
Material possessions, cheerful fans…
The healthy and free and fully alive innocent *Inner Child*
Deep within both of you has everything to do
With your genuine openness and receptivity
To each other:
★higher Self, originality, vulnerability, naivety...
★honesty, integrity, humility, infinite possibilities…
★true love, compassion, intimacy, higher creativity...

Their own Word

Poet Pablo Neruda said:

I love you without knowing how…
I love you simply...
I love you in this way because
I do not know any other way
of loving but this way in which
there is no I or you,. so intimate that
your hand in my chest is my hand.

Summary of the Chapter

Dear Spouses,
It is very difficult or even impossible
To have the will and skills and wisdom
You need
To love with true and long-lasting *Love,*
To be loved with true and long-lasting *Love,*
To enjoy and share true and long-lasting *Peace*
With each other,
To enjoy and share true and long-lasting *Intimacy*
With each other
When one or both of you face the faceless face
Of the disowned, the wounded, the silenced...
Innocent Inner Child
Deep within one or both of you.
The healthy and free and fully alive
Innocent *Inner Child* deep within both of you
Is the first vital but too often missing
Life-Saving Signal
On your long and rocky and slippery road

To true and long-lasting:

★love for each other,

★peace with each other,

★intimacy with each other.

Dear spouses, are you willing to fight with all your might to know why and how to:

- ★ *listen to your own small and still yet powerful Inner Voice?*
- ★ *listen to each other's small and still yet powerful Inner Voice?*
- ★ *listen to each other's loud but too often unheard cry for:*
  1. *ultimate meaning?*
  2. *healthy self-love, inner peace, inner autonomy?*
  3. *true love and long-lasting peace and intimacy with each other?*

- ★ are you willing to know why and how to enjoy and share *Oneness* with one another without losing your personal identity?

If *Yes* is your answer, you then may also need to know why and how to:

- ★ *be aware of the true nature and deep needs of your innocent Inner Child,*
- ★ *accept, respect, and protect the vulnerable innocent Inner Child in both of you,*
- ★ *accept, respect, and protect each other's innocent Inner Child deep needs.*

Your healthy and free and fully alive innocent *Inner Child* is your first *Vital* but often missing *Life Saving Signal* on your long, rocky, and slippery road to:

- ★ *healthy self-love,*
- ★ *true and long-lasting love for each other,*
- ★ *true and long-lasting peace and intimacy with each other.*

You need to be in touch with and deeply touched by your own healthy and free and fully alive innocent *Inner Child* if you are to know why and how to:

- ★ *read each other as you read a romance novel,*
- ★ *feel each other's deep feelings,*
- ★ *understand each other's fundamental but often hidden needs.*

Their own Words

Depth psychologist and psychoanalyst,
Carl G. Jung said:

In every adult lurks an inner child,
something that is always becoming,
something that is never completed,
something that is calling for incessant
caring, attention, education...

Anyone and anything can hurt your highly vulnerable innocent *Inner Child.*

As loving spouses, you can easily wound each other's vulnerable innocent *Inner Child.*

As feeble, fallible, and vulnerable human beings, you can easily disown and wound your own and each other's innocent *Inner Child.*

A wounded innocent *Inner Child* is a major barrier to your will, skills, and wisdom to know why and how to:

- ★ *love your own self with healthy self-love,*
- ★ *love each other with true and long-lasting love,*
- ★ *enjoy and share true and long-lasting peace and intimacy.*

Dear spouses, you need to know why and how to:

- ★ *be in love with your own true Self first if you are to be in love with each other,*
- ★ *be in peace with your own true Self first if you are to be in peace with each other,*
- ★ *be intimate with your own true Self first if you are to be intimate with each other.*

The deeper in touch you are with your own true *Self,* the deeper in touch you will be with each other's true *Self.* And the greater will be your opportunity to:

- ★ *accept, respect, and tolerate each other's natural difference,*
- ★ *forgive, forget, heal, be whole, enjoy and share a meaningful life...*
- ★ *treasure each other's Priceless Inner Treasure that is in no other.*

As loving spouses, you need to know why and how to meet and meltdown and be *One* with one another without losing your personal identity.

When you lose, for any reason, your personal identity, you have little or nothing worthy left on the inside.

Dear spouses,
Your Outer World,
compared to your Inner World,
is what the Earth is to the Solar System,
just a tiny and tinny part of an infinite whole.

The Problem

Dear spouses, the first major barrier to true *Love* and long-lasting *Peace* and *Intimacy* every loving spouse needs to know is the negative consequence of:

- ★ *the disowned innocent Inner Child in one or both of you,*
- ★ *the wounded innocent Inner Child in one or both spouses,*
- ★ *the silenced innocent Inner Child in one or both of you.*

The wounded innocent *Inner Child* within one or both of you is due to:

- ★ *one of the parenting 3 massive mistakes,*
- ★ *the Inner Child's elusive existence and vulnerability,*
- ★ *the Inner Child's deep needs and ultimate longings.*

For instance, you cannot see your own and each other's innocent *Inner Child.*

You cannot touch and manipulate your own and each other's innocent *Inner Child.*

Your innocent *Inner Child* has little or nothing to do with your:

- ★ *high academic achievement or vast practical skills…*
- ★ *celebrity, popularity or lack of them…*
- ★ *name, fame, fortune, cheerful fans or lack of them...*

The Solution

Your innocent *Inner Child* has everything to do with your:

- ★ *spiritual love, healthy self-love, unconditional love...*
- ★ *forgiveness, healing, wholeness, ultimate meaning...*
- ★ *honesty, integrity, humility, compassion, infinite possibilities...*

To enjoy and share your healthy, free and fully alive innocent *Inner Child,* you need to be aware of:

- ★ *the elusive nature of the innocent Inner Child within both of you,*
- ★ *the vulnerability of the innocent Inner Child within both of you,*
- ★ *the deep needs and ultimate longings of the innocent Inner Child within both of you.*

Be Aware of the Disowned innocent Inner Child

It is easy to disown the innocent *Inner Child.*

A disowned innocent *Inner Child* in one or both of you is what breaks your marriage from the inside out.

A disowned innocent *Inner Child* in one or both of you is a major barrier to:

- ★ *honesty, integrity, humility...in your marriage,*

- ★ *compassion, passion, intimacy...in your marriage,*
- ★ *inner peace and peace with each other...in your marriage.*

Imagine a marriage where there is no honesty, no integrity, no humility, no compassion, no peace, no intimacy...

It's *Hell* on *Earth.*

It takes forgiveness, healing, and wholeness of both of you to build a stable and happy...marriage.

Be Aware of the Inner Child's Extreme Vulnerability

When healthy, free, and fully alive, your *Inner Child* is one of your lifelong best friends.

When disowned, your innocent *Inner Child* is one of your lifelong worst enemies.

When it comes to the innocent *Inner Child,*
the dictum is:

There is nothing to do
and there is nowhere to go.
(Hal Stone and Sidarta, psychoanalysts)

That is how delicate is the innocent *Inner Child* within both of you.

That is how difficult it is to deal with the innocent *Inner Child* within both of you.

Depth psychologists characterize
the innocent Inner Child as:

The most disowned self in our civilized world.

The loss of the innocent *Inner Child* in one or both of you is at the root cause of some of your marriage's worst issues.

When one or both of you lose your healthy innocent *Inner Child*, you lose so much of the delight of your:

- ★ *healthy self-love, playfulness, humility...*
- ★ *spontaneity, vulnerability, naivety, intimacy...*
- ★ *originality, sociability, compassion, passion...*

Dear spouses,
One of the first biggest and most costly mistakes
in marriage is to fall in love with and marry each other's
natural and normal but too often too superficial Persona-mask
at the detriment of each other's true and total Personality.

Depth psychologist, Carl G. Jung, characterizes *the Persona-mask* as simple:

- ★ *masquerade,*
- ★ *or facade,*
- ★ *or social wrapping.*

Your true and total *Personality* is what you need if you are to know why and how to admit your personal mistakes and say honestly to each other:

- ★ *I made a mistake,*
- ★ *I am so sorry,*
- ★ *please, forgive me.*

The larger the gap between your *Persona-mask* and your *true and total Personality,* the greater your marriage risk of:

- ★ *infidelities,*
- ★ *instabilities,*
- ★ *possible divorce.*

Dear spouses, if you are not in touch with your own healthy innocent

Inner Child, you may often create what Carl G. Jung calls *the Empty Center.*

- In *the Empty Centre,* all you have is: *I, me, mine, myself...*
- *my way or no other way,*
- *megalomania, self-aggrandizement, vindictiveness, aggressiveness...*

In *the Empty Center,* your main preoccupation is:

- *does it work?*
- *what is in it for me?*
- *how can I get the best and the most out of what I want?*

If you are to enjoy and share a happy marriage, you need to know why and how to:

- *be open and receptive to each other's innocent Inner Child,*
- *feel each other's deep feelings,*
- *accept, respect, and protect each other's innocent Inner Child.*

Be Aware of the Wounded innocent Inner Child

Anyone can wound your innocent *Inner Child.*

Your loving and caring parents may have already wounded your innocent *Inner Child* long before you got married.

Children victims of one of the parenting 3 massive mistakes may face what Otto Rank and Carl G. Jung call:

- *the Fear of Life (Otto Rank),*
- *the Fear of Death (Otto Rank),*
- *the Empty Center (Carl G. Jung).*

Some of your teachers, classmates, coaches and teammates, friends and foes with their own wounded innocent *Inner Child* may have already wounded your innocent *Inner Child* long before you got married.

The ugly, dark, and stubborn side of your *personal Unconscious* is not easy to acknowledge and integrate into your *Conscious attitudes.*

When healthy, free, and fully alive, the innocent *Inner Child* within both of you has all the potentialities for:

- ★ *true love, aliveness, honesty, integrity, humility, impartiality...*
- ★ *forgiveness, healing, wholeness, a meaningful, peaceful, purposeful life...*
- ★ *compassion, passion, big dreams, higher creativity...*

Their own Words

In her book, *Reclaiming the Inner Child,*
Jeremiah Abrams said:

We always encounter the inner child in marriage
and other close associations with others,
where the wounding love of our past relationships
are the most deeply felt.
"The childhood wound to the soul,"
says Robert M. Stein, "makes it extremely difficult,
if not impossible, for one to experience an intimate
and creatively evolving human connection."

Your healthy, free, and fully alive innocent *Inner Child* may often tell you without any previous experience or rational explanation:

- ★ *who is who?*
- ★ *who is trustworthy and who is not?*
- ★ *who is more likely to hurt you because of their own hurting Inner Child.*

Be Aware of the Innocent Inner Child's Deep Needs

Your *Inner Child's* deep needs and ultimate longings have little or nothing to do with:

- ★ *beauty, charm, elegance...*
- ★ *deep knowledge, vast practical skills, well-paying jobs...*

- ★ *celebrity, popularity, fancy cars, gorgeous houses, name, fame, cheerful fans...*

Yes, beauty, charm, elegance, material abundance are all *Vital* to the quality and comfort of our day-to-day life.

No one can reasonably deny it.

For instance, as the novelist, JK. Rowling---
commonly-known as Henry Potter---said during
her Commencement Speech at Harvard University:

Only a fool can romanticize poverty.

But the Scriptures also ask the following life learning
and life-changing question to anyone with a thinking soul:

What do you have
when you gain the whole world
but lose your own soul?

For all true believers, *Nothing* is the most obvious answer.

Your healthy, free, and fully alive innocent *Inner Child's* deep needs and ultimate longings have everything to do with your true and long-lasting:

- ★ *healthy self-love and infinite possibilities...*
- ★ *inner peace, inner autonomy, peace with each other, peace with almost all...*
- ★ *divine/spiritual love, unconditional love for all including your worst enemies.*

Their own Words

Psychoanalyst, Alice Miller, said:

Only when I make room for the voice
of the child within me, do I feel myself
to be genuine and creative.

Dear spouse,
It is better to lie to the whole world
than lying to your own self.
If you lie to your own self,
you may lie to everyone else.
If you are true to your own true Self,
you may be true to everyone else.

To "Thine Self Be True"

Hollywood producer, Samuel Golden said:

It is not a secret, I never attended Havard or Oxford.

The only formal education I ever had was the little I acquired
at night while I was working in a factory during day time.

I am not a Shakespearian too.

But I always considered:
"To thine own self be true" as the soundest
possible guide to a successful living.

And when I say successful living, I mean it in every sense of the word.

In all the years I have been in Hollywood, I have one basic piece of advice
for the actors and actresses...

"Be yourself."

That is my own way of saying:

"To thine own self be true."

Once one has fully entered the realm of love,
the world...no matter how imperfect...
becomes rich and beautiful...
(S. Kierkergard, theologian)

Dear spouses,
Before and beyond your beauty and charm and elegance,
Before and beyond your deep knowledge and vast practical skills,
Before and beyond your well paying job and financial stability,
Your healthy and free and fully alive innocent *Inner Child*
Deep within both of you
Is
Your first wide-open door to *the realm of love.*

CHAPTER 2

Fulfill The Inner Void

Step 2

Dear spouses, ***Step 2*** *to true Love and long-lasting Peace and Intimacy every loving spouse needs to know is why and how to enjoy and share true and long-lasting* ***Fulfillment.***

Dear spouses,
The parenting second massive mistake
Or teens, adolescents, and young adults' way as almost the only way,
Or what the psychologist, Otto Rank, calls *the Fear of Death*
Is a major barrier to true *Love* and long-lasting *Peace and Intimacy.*
When one or both of you are more focused on
Your second deepest need for relative *Independence*
At the detriment of your first deepest need for *Belonging,*
You undermine and compromise your openness and receptivity
To the *Larger* than *Life deep within and all around both of you.*

Your true and long-lasting *Fulfillment* is vital to your:
★*healthy self-love, inner peace, inner autonomy...*
★*true and long-lasting love for each other,*
★*true and long-lasting peace and intimacy with each other.*

Your true and long-lasting *Fulfillment* requires
★*divine/spiritual love, healthy self-love, unconditional love,*
★*forgiveness, healing, wholeness, ultimate meaning, inner peace,*
★*the emergence of each other's true, transcendent, infinite Self.*

Your religious and spiritual traditions and collective wisdom
Have been telling you all along with that:

⋆you each are created at God-image,
⋆you each are created at God-likeness,
⋆God is all-loving, all-knowing, all-powerful.
The larger the gap between who you are divinely/spiritually
Meant to be
And whom you happen to be in your day-to-day life,
The deeper your unfathomable and unbearable *Inner Void.*

Their own Words

Pre-Socratic philosopher, Sophocle, said:

One word frees us of all
the weight and pain of life.
That word is love.

Dear spouses,
The second *Vital* but too often missing *Life-Saving Signal*
On the long road to true *Love* and long-lasting *Peace* and *Intimacy*
Every loving spouse needs to know
Is
The powerful life-giving and life animating power
Of true and long-lasting
FULFILLMENT
For both of you.

You cannot enjoy and share true and long-lasting:
**love for each other,*
**peace with each other,*
**intimacy with each other*
When one or both of you face the faceless face
Of the deep and unfathomable
INNER VOID.

The second *Vital* but too often missing *Life-Saving Signal*
On your long road to true *Love* and long-lasting *Peace* and *Intimacy*
You need to know
Is
Your ever-increasing and never-ending striving
To know why and how to enjoy and share
True and long-lasting *Fulfillment.*

Dear spouses,
The best would be loving spouses among you
May not know why and how
To enjoy and share true and long lasting:
**love for each other,*
**peace with each other,*
**intimacy with each other*
When one or both of you face the faceless face
Of the deep and unfathomable possible
INNER VOID.

No deep knowledge, no vast practical skills,
No power position, no material possessions,
No name, no fame, no celebrity, no popularity...
Can help you *Fulfill* the deep and unfathomable
INNER VOID
Within one or both of you.

Only divine love, healthy self-love,
Spiritual love, unconditional love,
Forgiveness, healing, wholeness, ultimate meaning,
Inner peace...
Can help you *Fulfill* the deep and unfathomable
INNER VOID
Within one or both of *you*.

Their own Word

Theologian and philosopher,
Meister Eckhart said:

One person who has mastered life
is better than a thousand persons
who have mastered only the content of books,
but no one can get anything out of life
without God.

Summary of the Chapter,

Dear Spouses,
It is very difficult or even impossible
To have the will and skills and wisdom
You need
To love with true and long-lasting *Love,*
To be loved with true and long-lasting *Love,*
To enjoy and share true and long-lasting *Peace*
With each other,
To enjoy and share true and long-lasting *Intimacy*
With each other
When one or both of you face the faceless face
Of the deep and unfathomable
Inner Void
Deep within one or both of you.
If you are to love truly,
If you are to be loved truly
With true and long-lasting *Love,*
With true and long-lasting *Peace*
With each other,
With true and long lasting-*Intimacy*
With each other,

You need to know why and how
To be deeply in touch with,
To be deeply touched by
The *Larger* than *Life* deep within both of you,
The *Larger* than *Life* all around both of you,
The *Larger* than *Life* in between
The best there is
Deep within and all around both of you.

Dear spouses, are you willing to fight with all your might to know why and how to:

- ★ *enjoy true and long-lasting Fulfillment?*
- ★ *share true and long-lasting Fulfillment?*
- ★ *celebrate true and-long lasting Fulfillment?*

If *Yes* is your answer, you then need also to know why and how to:

- ★ *be deeply in touch with the Larger than Life deep within you,*
- ★ *be deeply touched by the Larger than Life all around you,*
- ★ *enjoy and share the Larger than Life within and all around both of you.*

The ineffable presence of the *Larger than Life* deep within and all around both of you is *Vital* to your true and long-lasting *Fulfillment.*

True and long-lasting *Fulfillment* is part of what you need if you are to know why and how to:

- ★ *love truly, live fully alive, forgive, forget, heal, be whole...*
- ★ *be open and receptive to ultimate meaning or meaning as divine design...*
- ★ *enjoy and share strong belief systems and solid worldviews...*

True love, forgiveness, healing, wholeness, strong belief systems ...are important to your marriage's stability.

Your spiritually way of being is part of your pathways to the *Larger* than *Life:*

- ★ *deep within you,*
- ★ *all around you,*
- ★ *in between the best there is within and all around both of you.*

If you are not open and receptive to the *Larger* than *Life* deep within and all around both of you, your marriage may face the faceless face of the ineffable and unbearable *Pain* of what Viktor E. Frankl calls:

- ★ *the existential vacuum,*

- ★ *the existential frustration,*
- ★ *the frustrated will to meaning, to power, to money, and to pleasure at its lowest level.*

A marriage without true and long-lasting *Love and Peace and Intimacy* is often due, to some degree, to one or both spouses' lack of a strong belief system or spiritual way of being or solid worldviews or shared values or time-tested ways of life...

Your marriage's stability requires more than what is going on in your day-to-day material world.

That is why marriage's issues may knock on all doors, including the doors of:

- ★ *the most powerful,*
- ★ *the very rich,*
- ★ *the most famous.*

The Problem

Dear spouses, the second major barrier to true *Love* and long lasting *Peace and Intimacy* every loving spouse needs to know is why and how to:

- ★ prevent the deep and unfathomable *Inner Void* within one of both of you,
- ★ or confront the deep and unfathomable *Inner Void* within one or both of you,
- ★ *and overcome* the deep and unfathomable *Inner Void* within one or both of you.

The deep and unfathomable possible *Inner Void* is due to the lack of *Alignment* with the *Spirit or the Divine Order.*

The *meaning* of life and the *meaning* of your own life, your *Fulfillment*, your *Inner Peace* and your *Peace* with each other, and your possible

Peace with everyone else may be as vital to your marriage's stability as your needs for:

★ *fresh air to breath,*
★ *healthy food to eat and clean water to drink,*
★ *a roof and a room and a place to call home.*

Some of the world great religious and spiritual traditions and collective wisdom have been telling us that:

★ *we each and all are created at God-image,*
★ *we each and all are created at God-likeness,*
★ *God is all-loving, all-knowing, all-powerful.*

For true believers, that means that we each and all are divinely/ spiritually meant to be:

★ *all-loving,*
★ *all-knowing,*
★ *all-powerful.*

What a powerful life-giving and life animating power!

How inspiring and uplifting it is to be aware and convinced that there is always:

★ *something more,*
★ *something bigger,*
★ *something better.*

But, our day-to-day life inevitable *Conflicts,* our natural and normal pairs of personal inner *Opposites*, and our possible fears, failures, lacks, and temporary setbacks are also telling us that we each and all are merely:

★ *what we know,*
★ *what we do,*
★ *what we have.*

When one or both of you face the faceless face of the deep and unfathomable *Inner Void*, no one and nothing material can help you *Fulfill it:*

- ★ *no deep knowledge, no vast practical skills, no well-paying jobs...*
- ★ *no name, no fame, no celebrity, no popularity, no cheerful fans...*
- ★ *no food, no alcohol, no drug, no sex...addiction...*

The deep *Inner Void* within one or both of you may drag your marriage into what neurologist, psychiatrist, and logo-therapist, Viktor E. Frankl, calls:

- ★ *the existential vacuum,*
- ★ *the existential frustration,*
- ★ *the frustrated will to meaning, to power, to money, to pleasure at its lowest level.*

The Existential Vacuum

Imagine how *frustrated someone can be* when experiencing the *Empty Center.*

In the *Empty Center,* there are no shared values, no solid worldviews, no philosophies of life.

In the *Empty Center,* all there is is:

- ★ *I, me, mine, myself...*
- ★ *my own way or no other way...*
- ★ *self-aggrandizement, megalomania...*

It will be hard for spouses victims of the *Empty Center* to know why and how to enjoy and share true and long-lasting:

- ★ *love with each other,*
- ★ *peace with each other,*
- ★ *intimacy with each other.*

The *Existential Vacuum* defies deep knowledge, vast practical skills, extraordinary success.

The Existential Vacuum may happen to anyone who is not open and receptive to *Ultimate Meaning or Spiritually integrated ways of being.*

Imagine the feeling of hopelessness and helplessness of a living without:

- ★ *Ultimate Meaning,*
- ★ *or Super-Meaning,*
- ★ *or Meaning as Divine Design.*

The Existential Frustration

Existential Frustration may also happen to anyone.

It may happen to the poor as well as to the rich and to the famous.

There are people who are fighting with all their might for a decent living.

But a decent living alone does not necessarily guarantee a meaningful life.

Yes, there is no life without a living.

But there is more to life than a mere living.

A mere living is about material things and leisure and pleasure.

A meaningful life is about man's deep needs and ultimate longings.

For instance, we each have deep needs and ultimate longings for true and long lasting:

- ★ *love, inner peace, peace with one another...*
- ★ *a peaceful life in a peaceful world for every thinking soul...*
- ★ *a fulfilled life or true and long-lasting joy for no tangible reason...*

You may have known and seen or heard about world-famous stars in sport, in music, in the movie industry...who, despite their talent, name and fame and fortune and cheerful fans, are living a meaningless and lifeless life because of:

- ★ *their alcohol addiction,*
- ★ *their drug addiction,*
- ★ *their opioid addiction.*

Their own Story

"You Never Know"

Prisoner no 174517 was incarcerated in one
of the Nazi's extermination Camps,
at Auschwitz, Poland.

One day, he was thirsty.

He saw a fat icicle hanging outside of the hut.
He broke the window to quench his thirst.

But before he could get the icicle in his mouth, a prison guard
snatched it out of his hand and tossed it to the ground.

"Wharum" which means "why" in German, asked the prisoner.

"Hier ist kein wharum" which means "here, there is no why,"
answered the prison guard.

The name of the prisoner number 174517 was Primo Levi,
an Italian Jew.

Primo was a scientist and a writer.

After that incident, Primo concluded that,
"never again" was a too confident assertion.

Therefore, Primo suggested that "you never know" has to be the refrain.

Primo was one of the 3 survivors of a group of 650 Jews transported to Poland in 1944.

Upon his release, Primo got married. Primo got children. Primo wrote books. Primo won literary prizes...

But one day, in April 1987, more than 40 years after his release from Auschwitz concentration Camp, Primo plunged to his death down the stairwell of his home, in Torino, Italy.

After 40 years, Primo has not forgotten and forgiven what has happened to him at Auschwitz?

Primo had a clean-cut picture of his self-identity.
Primo had a passionate life. Yet, he committed suicide.
He did it more likely because of his lack of solid faith
and true and long-lasting Ultimate Meaning in life.
(re-adapted from Os Guinness's book "Long Journey HOME:
A Guide to Your Search for the Meaning of life."

Solution

The tragic story of Primo Levi is living proof that to survive and thrive, we human beings need the meaning of life and the meaning of our own personal life.

We need to know why and how to enjoy and share our need for *Belonging* if we are to know why and how to:

- ★ *love truly and live fully alive...*
- ★ *forgive, forget, heal, be whole...*
- ★ *celebrate a meaningful life in a meaningful world for every thinking soul...*

To prevent or confront and overcome the deep and unfathomable *Inner Void,* every loving spouse needs to know why and how to enjoy and share:

- ★ *divine love, divine grace, divine guidance...*
- ★ *forgiveness, healing, wholeness, a meaningful life, the emergence of the true Self...*
- ★ *healthy self-love, spiritual love, unconditional love...*

All loving spouses need to know why and how to be in touch with the *Larger* than *Life* if they are to know why and how to prevent or overcome:

- ★ *the deep and ineffable possible Inner Void,*
- ★ *the deep and unfathomable possible Inner Void,*
- ★ *the deep and unbearable possible Inner Void.*

Their own Words

Psychiatrist, depth psychologist, and
psychoanalyst, Carl G. Jung, said:

No one knows what the ultimate things are. We must therefore take them as we experience them. And if such experience helps to make life healthier, more beautiful, more complete, and more satisfactory

to yourself and those you love, you may safely say:
"This was the grace of God."

Dear spouses, to overcome the faceless face of *the Existential Vacuum*, the *Existential Frustration*, and the *Frustrated Will to Meaning, to Power, to Money, to Pleasure at its lowest level*, you need to know why and how to listen to, understand, internalize and co-own what your world great religious and spiritual traditions and collective wisdom have been telling you all along about:

- *life, love, true and long-lasting inner peace, peace with one another...*
- *ultimate meaning or meaning as divine design...*
- *happiness in life and in marriage...*

Your healthy self-love, spiritual love, and unconditional love are vital components to the *Solution* to your:

- *life inevitable Conflicts,*
- *natural and normal pairs of personal inner Opposites,*
- *marriage's possible Challenges.*

It takes a strong belief system and moral courage and effort to integrate the dark and ugly and stubborn side of your *personal Unconscious* into your *Conscious* attitudes.

Yet, that is the way to go if you are to know why and how to enjoy and share:

- *true and long-lasting Inner Peace so vital to your Peace with each other,*
- *honesty, integrity, humility, compassion, passion, intimacy...*
- *subjectivity, originality, spontaneity, vulnerability, naivety...*

Forgiveness

You need to know how to love truly and live fully alive if you are to know why and how to:

- *forgive and forget,*

- ★ *heal and be whole,*
- ★ *enjoy and share a meaningful life, a peaceful life, a purposeful life...*

Their own Story

The late Dr.Wayne Dyer is a well known bestselling author,
a spiritual guru and a motivational speaker.

But his life has not always been on the rosy side of the road.

He has had his own lion share of frustration
and resentment and bitterness.

But he had also learned why and how to love truly, live fully alive,
forgive, forget, heal, be whole...

Dr. Dyer said:
My old man, ...walked out of my life when I was an infant.
He never came back. He never even bothered to call me back.

My old man drank excessively. He was abusive of mom…
He spent some time in prison.

He died of cirrhosis of the liver at the age of forty-nine.
He was buried in a pauper's grave, in Biloxi, Mississippi.

I carried the burden of resentment, hatred, and bitterness till my early thirty.

Then, I went to his grave and said essentially the same thing
that poet Langston Hughes said:

"I take my curse back."

In doing so, I literally transformed my life.

My writing began to click. My approach to my health improves significantly...most of all I felt free from having the venom of resentment and hatred pumping through my veins...

When we learn to forgive, we rise above those who insult us.

The act of forgiveness put an end to the quarrel.

Every hurt...is like a snake bite...once bitten it is impossible to be unbitten…the damage is done by the venom that continues to flow through your system…The venom is your bitterness that you hang on to, too long after you have been bitten.

It is the venom of bitterness that destroys your peace of mind.

We each have our own personal issues, let alone when we are two persons in a close and intimate relationship such as marriage.

We sleep with men but rest only when alone
with that ineffable something in us greater
than us and larger than life.
(Rumi, poet)

Dear spouses, true and long lasting *Fulfillment* is your *Second Vital* but too often missing *Step* on your long road to true and long lasting:

- ★ *love for each other,*
- ★ *peace with each other,*
- ★ *intimacy with each other.*

To love truly and live fully alive, you need to be in touch with your own and with each other:

- ★ *true Self,*
- ★ *transcendent Self,*
- ★ *infinite Self.*

The emergence of your own true *Self* is the *Solution* to the deep and unfathomable *Inner Void* or what Viktor E. Frankl calls:

- ★ *the existential vacuum,*
- ★ *the existential frustration,*
- ★ *the frustrated will to meaning...*

Russian writer, Ivan Turgenev, is reported having said that he would trade all his art and all his books for the joy of knowing that someone, his spouse, is worried because he is late for dinner.

Dear spouses,
Are you willing to know why and how
To enjoy and share true and long-lasting:
★*love for each other?*
★*peace with each other?*
★*intimacy with each other?*
Are you willing to trade wholeheartedly
What is near and dear
To your heart and soul and spirit
For the joy of knowing why and how
To enjoy and share true and long-lasting:
★*love for each other?*
★*peace with each other?*
★*intimacy with each other?*
That's your second *Vital* but too often missing
Life-Saving Signal
On your long and rocky and slippery road
To true *Love*
And long-lasting *Peace* and *Intimacy* with each other.

CHAPTER 3

End The Empty Center

Step 3

*Dear spouses, **Step 3** to true Love and long-lasting Peace*
and Intimacy every loving spouse needs to know is why and
*how to **Prevent** or **Confront** and **Overcome** the ineffable and*
*unbearable **Pain of Inner Emptiness** within one or both of you.*

Dear spouses,
The parenting third massive mistake
Or *parents and their teens, adolescents and young adults*
With no common way or no way at all
Pushes certain teens, adolescents, and young adults
To create what depth psychologist, Carl G. Jung, calls:
THE EMPTY CENTER.
In the *Empty Center*, there are no solid worldviews,
No philosophies of life,
No shared values, no time-tested ways of life...

In *the Empty Center*, all there is is:
★*I, me, mine, myself...*
★*my own way or no other way...*
★*self aggrandizement, megalomania...*
In the *Empty Center*, the main focus
Of the domineering spouse is:
★*does it work?*
★*what is in it for me?*
★*how can I get the best and the most out of what I want?*

A spouse with the *Empty Center* makes life miserable
To the other spouse, constrained to either leave or endure
A meaningless and lifeless life in a miserable marriage.
To overcome the ineffable and unbearable *Pain of Inner Emptiness*
Requires deep soul searching, moral courage, and effort.
That is what it takes to integrate the dark
and ugly and stubborn side
Of one or both spouses' *Personal Unconscious*
Into their Conscious attitudes;
Integration so vital to their *Inner Freedom,*
Inner Peace and true Peace and *Intimacy* with one another.

Their own Words

Dr. Malick Kouyate, the co-founder of
All For Excellence In Education (AFEIE), said:

The Pain of Inner Emptiness is ineffable and unbearable. No one and nothing material can alleviate the Pain of Inner Emptiness. Only divine/ spiritual love, healthy self-love, unconditional love, forgiveness, healing, wholeness, ultimate meaning...can prevent or help confront and overcome the ineffable and unbearable ***Pain of Inner Emptiness.***

Dear spouses,
The third *Vital* but too often missing *Life Saving Signal*
On the long road to true *Love* and long-lasting *Peace and Intimacy*
Every loving spouse needs to know
Is
The powerful life-giving and life animating power
Of knowing why and how to enjoy and share true and long-lasting
INNER PEACE
So vital to true and long-lasting *Peace* and *Intimacy* with each other.

You cannot enjoy and share true and long-lasting:
**healthy self-love,*
**love for each other,*
**peace and intimacy with each other*
When one or both of you face the ineffable and unbearable pain of
INNER EMPTINESS.

The third *Vital* but too often missing *Life Saving Signal*
On the long road to true *Love* and long-lasting *Peace and Intimacy*
You need to know
Is
Your ever-increasing and never-ending striving

To know why and how to:
★identify your own true identity,
★be true to your own true identity,
★become who truly you are meant to be.
You have to be true to your own true Self
If you are to be true to anyone else
Including your loving spouse.

Dear spouses,
The best would be loving spouses among you
May not know why and how
To enjoy and share true and long-lasting:
★love for each other,
★peace with each other,
★intimacy with each other
When one or both of you face the faceless face
Of the ineffable and unbearable *Pain* of
INNER EMPTINESS.

If you are to prevent successfully,
Or confront constructively,
And overcome definitively
The ineffable and unbearable *Pain* of
INNER EMPTINESS
Within one or both of you,
You need to know why and how to:
★identify your own true identity,
★be true to your own true identity,
★become who truly you are meant to be.

Their Own Words

Depth psychologist and psychoanalyst,
Carl G. Jung said:

Acceptance of one's own inner Self
is the essence of the moral problem and
the acid test of one's whole outlook on life.

Summary of the Chapter

Dear Spouses,
It is very difficult or even impossible
To have the will and skills and wisdom
You need
To love with true and long-lasting *Love,*
To be loved with true and long-lasting *Love,*
To enjoy and share true and long-lasting *Peace*
With each other,
To enjoy and share true and long-lasting *Intimacy*
With each other
When one or both of you face the faceless face
Of the ineffable and unbearable
Pain of Inner Emptiness.
In the *Empty Center,*
You have no time tested ways of life,
You have no shared values,
You have no solid worldviews.
In the *Empty Center,* all you have
Is:
⋆*I, me, mine, myself...*
⋆*my way or no other way...*
⋆*self-aggrendisment, megalomania, aggressiveness…*

Imagine a marriage when one spouse
Has to dominate and control and dictate it all,
While the other spouse
Has to leave or to endure it all.

Dear spouses, are you willing to fight with all your might to know why and how to:

★ *welcome your own true Self?*
★ *enjoy and share each other's true Self?*
★ *celebrate true and long-lasting Peace and Intimacy with each other?*

If *Yes* is your answer, you then need also to know why and how to:

★ *identify your own true identity,*
★ *be true to your own true identity,*
★ *become who truly you are meant to be.*

You are always with your own self. But you may live your whole life without being in touch with and deeply touched by your own:

★ *true Self,*
★ *transcendent Self,*
★ *infinite Self.*

Dear spouses, you need to know why and how to love truly, live fully alive and forgive, forget, heal, be whole, enjoy and share the emergence of your own and each other's true *Self* if you are to know why and how to:

★ *love your own self with healthy self-love,*
★ *love each other with true and long-lasting love,*
★ *enjoy and share true and long-lasting peace and intimacy with each other.*

The larger the gap between your natural and normal *Persona-mask* and your *true and total Personality*, the deeper the wound you may inflict to anyone close to you including your own:

★ *loving spouse,*
★ *innocent children,*
★ *caring parents, brothers, sisters...*

In-depth self-discovery is one of your life's greatest discoveries.

In-depth self-discovery precedes and prepares your ability to:

- ★ *identify what you want most out of your life,*
- ★ *identify what you are most good at,*
- ★ *re-align what you have to do to what you are called to do.*

Dear spouses,
It is said that when your profession
coincides with your vocation,
the rest is illumination.

To succeed in life, you need to know, as early as possible, why and how to:

- ★ *identify your dominant talent,*
- ★ *be focused on your dominant talent,*
- ★ *build upon your dominant talent.*

You are meant to identify your dominant talent by and through some of your life learning and life-changing experiences.

For instance, if you have all the money you need to live a decent living for the rest of your life, what would you still be willing to do to solve for example some:

- ★ *educational issues in your community, county, country?*
- ★ *teaching-learning issues in your community, county, country?*
- ★ *marriage issues in your community, county, country?*

Your day-to-day struggle for material things is a natural and normal struggle.

You cannot survive and thrive without the minimum material needs.

Your hard work is a social and historical necessity.

But your hard work alone won't work for your longing for wholeness.

Along with your material needs, you need to know why and how to enjoy and share your spiritual needs.

The satisfaction of your spiritual needs is fundamental to the quality of your life and marriage.

Great success
without fulfillment is the ultimate failure.
(Tony Robbins, author, and motivational speaker)

Indeed, when you feel *Empty on the Inside*, you may have the whole world and still live a meaningless and lifeless life.

Dear spouses,
It is hard to live a meaningless life,
It is hard to live a lifeless life,
It is harder still to die while seemingly alive.

Yet, dying while seemingly alive is what is happening to many spouses of many different walks of life around many different corners of the world.

There are spouses who are fighting day and night for a more abundant life.

But an abundant life alone does not automatically guarantee a meaningful life.

You may have all the material you need and still feel *Empty* on the *Inside.*

You may not know what is missing. But you do know that something deep on the inside is not right. You feel what is missing on the inside even if you cannot name it or explain it…

The ineffable and unbearable missing *something more and bigger and better* is what is dragging so many spouses into the bottomless abyss of nothingness.

Dear spouses,
A living, including a decent living,
without a meaningful life,
is not worth living.

Your true and long-lasting *Inner Peace* so vital to your true and long-lasting *Peace* with each other is fundamental to your openness and receptivity to:

- ★ *ultimate meaning,*
- ★ *or super-meaning,*
- ★ *or meaning as divine design.*

Your true and long-lasting *Inner Peace* is one of the rock-solid founding and building blocks of your true and long-lasting:

- ★ *healthy self-love,*
- ★ *love for each other,*
- ★ *peace and intimacy with each other.*

Dear spouses,
If you are to enjoy and share
True and long-lasting:
**love for each other,*
**peace with each other,*
**intimacy with each other*
You need to know why and how to:
**awaken the positive side of the Sleeping Giant in you that is in no other,*
**treasure the Priceless Inner Treasure in you that is in no other,*
**sing the life most favorite Love Song in you*
that has never been sung before.

Your lifelong most favorable love song
may just be your innocent smile
So much in need by
so many innocent children.

To succeed in your life and in your marriage,
You need to know why and how
To be true to your own true *Identity.*
On the one hand, you are unique,
On the other hand, you are *One*
With all the men and all the women
Of the whole world,
Who each and all are the same important members
Of the same important *Family: the Human Family.*

Their own Words

Ralph Waldo Emerson, the architect
of the transcendentalist movement
in Boston, said:

What lies in front of us
and what lies behind us
are small matters
compared to what lies
within us.

Dear spouse, there has never been someone exactly like you.

There will never be someone exactly like you.

To some degree, you are unique.

You are made to make a difference in your own life and in the lives of your loved ones and important others.

You are more.

You are more than your academic achievement.

You are more than your job description and paycheck.

You are more than what you know and do and have combined.

You are more than your fears, failures, lacks and temporary setbacks.

You are more than your celebrity and popularity.

You are more than your name and fame and fortune.

You are more than your power position and material possessions.

You are more than your fancy cars and gorgeous houses.

You are, to some degree, a spiritual being.

You have some deep needs and ultimate longings no one and nothing material can help you satisfy.

He Who is in you is greater than he who is in the world.
(Christianity)

The Problem

Dear spouses, the third major barrier to true *Love* and long-lasting *Peace* and *Intimacy* every loving spouse needs to know is why and how to:

- ★ *prevent the ineffable and unbearable Pain of Inner Emptiness,*
- ★ *or confront the ineffable and unbearable Pain of Inner Emptiness,*
- ★ *and overcome the ineffable and unbearable Pain of Inner Emptiness.*

The unbearable possible *Pain of Inner Emptiness* is due to what Jung calls the *Empty Center.*

The *Empty Center* is due to:

- ★ *the parenting third massive mistake,*
- ★ *the dark and ugly and stubborn side of the Personal Unconscious,*
- ★ *the gap between the Persona-mask and the true and total Personality.*

The *Empty Center* has a lot to do with what Viktor E. Frankl calls:

- ★ *the frustrated will to Meaning,*
- ★ *the frustrated will to Power,*
- ★ *the frustrated will to Money,*
- ★ *the frustrated will to Pleasure at its lowest level.*

Meaning, power, material abundance, and a life full of socially induced pleasure and leisure...are all vital to the quality and comfort in our day-to-day life.

But the frustrated *Will to Meaning, to Power, to Money, and to Pleasure* at its lowest level is probably the world wide most spread *Frustration.* It involves so many different people of so many different social and cultural backgrounds from so many different countries.

The frustrated Will to Meaning, to Power, to Money and to Pleasure at its lowest level may knock on all doors, including the doors of:

- ⋆ *the well educated,*
- ⋆ *the most powerful,*
- ⋆ *the rich and the famous.*

Dear spouses,
The Frustrated Will to Meaning
May not necessarily lead you
To true and long-lasting Meaning,
The Frustrated Will to Power
May not necessarily lead you
To true and long lasting Power,
The Frustrated Will to Money,
May not necessarily lead you
To true and long-lasting Wealth,
The Frustrated Will to Pleasure,
May not necessarily lead you
To true and long-lasting Intimacy.

The Solution

The *Solution* to the ineffable and unbearable *Pain of Inner Emptiness* is to inspire each other to know why and how to enjoy and share the emergence of your respective:

- ⋆ *true Self,*
- ⋆ *transcendent Self,*
- ⋆ *infinite Self.*

The emergence of your true, transcendent, infinite *Self* is *crucial* to the success of your struggle for a living conducive to *Ultimate Meaning or Super-Meaning or Meaning as Divine Design.*

True and long lasting *Inner Peace* is the *Panacea* or universal remedy against your:

- ★ *bitterness, resentment, guilty feelings...*
- ★ *alcohol, drug, opioid, food, sex addiction...*
- ★ *domestic violence and man-made tragedies.*

But true and long lasting *Inner Peace* requires the *Harmony* between your natural and normal pairs of *personal Inner Opposites,* such as your:

- ★ *Consciousness and Unconscious,*
- ★ *Ego and Shadow,*
- ★ *Persona-mask and true and total Personality.*

You need true and long lasting *Inner Peace* with your own true *Self* if you are to be in *Peace* with anyone else starting by your ow:

- ★ *spouse,*
- ★ *children,*
- ★ *parents, brothers, sisters, intimate friends, co-workers.*

Peace with your own true *Self* is the third *Vital* but too often missing *Life Saving Signal* on your long and often rocky and slippery road to true and long-lasting:

- ★ *love for each other,*
- ★ *peace with each other,*
- ★ *intimacy with each other.*

The ineffable and unbearable *Pain of Inner Emptiness* is a major barrier to:

- ★ *the positive side of the Sleeping Giant within every one of you,*
- ★ *the Priceless Inner Treasure within every one of you that is in no other,*
- ★ *the most favorite Love Song within every one of you that has never been sung before.*

If you want to prevent or confront and overcome the ineffable and unbearable possible *Pain of Inner Emptiness* in one or both of you, you need to know why and how to:

- ★ *identify your own true identity,*

- *be true to your own true identity,*
- *become who truly you are meant to be.*

To alleviate and eradicate the unbearable *Pain of Inner Emptiness*, you need to know why and how to:

- *love all those who love you,*
- *love even all those who hate you,*
- *forgive all those who hurt you,*
- *share the ineffable place deep within you where you are One with everyone.*

But no one and nothing material can help you alleviate the ineffable and unbearable *Pain of Inner Emptiness.* Only divine love, divine grace, divine guidance, healthy self-love, spiritual love, unconditional love, forgiveness, healing, wholeness, ultimate meaning can help you alleviate and eradicate the ineffable and unbearable *Pain of Inner Emptiness.*

To succeed, you need to know why and how to:

- *use the best in your "Outer World" to awaken the best there is in your "Inner World,"*
- *use the best there is in your "Inner World" to add meaning to your "Outer World,"*
- *tap into the magic between the best there is in your "Inner and Outer worlds."*

When you lose your true *Self,* you have *no Harmony* between your natural and normal pairs of personal *Inner Opposites.* When you lose your true *Self,* you have no other way to:

- *the meaning of the world you live in,*
- *the meaning of your own life in the world,*
- *the meaning of your own life destiny.*

Without true and long lasting *love, forgiveness, healing, wholeness, Inner Peace, Ultimate Meaning or Meaning as Divine Design,* you may feel:

- ★ *alone and lonely even in the midst of the noisiest crowds,*
- ★ *a stranger to anyone else, including to your own self,*
- ★ *an unlikeable and unlovable host in a hostile environment.*

PART II

How to Overcome the 3 States of Mind that Prevent Would be Loving Spouses from Knowing Why and How to Love Each Other with True Love and Long-Lasting Peace and Intimacy?

The outstanding intellectual need of our time is to get beyond the limitations of the nineteenth-century conception of human nature. It left us too restricted a view of life with its rationalistic economic man and its biological and historical determinism. [Now is the time] *to break free of the nineteenth century and find a larger vision of reality.*
(Ira Progoff, author of Jung's Psychology and its Social Implication),

Dear spouses,

The 3 limiting and misleading states of mind
That prevent would be loving spouses
From knowing why and how to:
★love their own self with healthy self-love,
★love each other with true and long-lasting love,
★enjoy and share true and long-lasting peace and intimacy
are:
★meaninglessness,
★mindlessness,
★shortsightedness.

These 3 limiting and misleading
States of mind are 3 major barriers to:
★ultimate meaning,
★mindfulness,
★the more than eye can see within both of you.

CHAPTER 4

Overcome Meaninglessness

Step 4

Dear spouses, ***Step 4*** *to true Love and long lasting Peace* and
*Intimacy every loving Spouse needs to know is why and how to tap into
the Powerful life-giving and life animating* ***Power*** *of* ***Ultimate Meaning***
or ***Super-Meaning*** *or* ***Meaning*** *as* ***Divine Design.***

Dear spouses,
Depth psychologists tell us that modern man's biggest problem
Is not a personality problem,
Modern man's biggest problem is a religious or spiritual problem,
Modern man's deepest need is the meaning of life
Modern man's deepest need is the meaning of his own life.

When one or both of you face the faceless face of *Meaninglessness,*
You go deep into the bottomless abyss of *Nothingness,*
Or what neurologist and logo-therapist, Viktor E. Frankl, calls:
**the existential vacuum,*
**the existential frustration,*
**the frustrated will to meaning, to power, to money, to pleasure.*
When one or both of you feel *Empty on the Inside,*
No one and nothing material or no worldly pleasure or leisure
Can help you face the ineffable and
unbearable Pain of *Inner Emptiness.*

Modern man is in search of the *meaning* of life,
Modern man is also in search of the *meaning* of his own life,
If he fail, it doesn't matter what else he finds in life,
He will be facing the faceless face of the ineffable and unbearable

Pain of Inner Emptiness.
To overcome the unbearable pain of *Inner Emptiness,*
Modern man needs to know why and how
to transcend *meaning* as simple:
★social construct,
★personal construct,
★dialogical encounter between social and personal construct.
To enjoy and share a meaningful life in a meaningful world
For every thinking soul, modern man needs to know why and how
To be open and receptive to *Ultimate Meaning*
Or Meaning as Divine Design.

Their own Words

Zen Buddhism's teaching said:

...the key to inner growth is...a wordless intuition
that there must be "something more,"
the pictures vary,
but the experiences point in the same direction.

Dear spouses,
The fourth *Vital* but too often missing *Life Saving Signal*
On the long road to true *Love* and long lasting *Peace and Intimacy*
Every loving spouse needs to know
Is
The powerful life-giving and animating power of
Ultimate Meaning.

You cannot enjoy and share true and long lasting:
**love for each other,*
**peace with each other,*
**intimacy with each other*
When one or both of you face the faceless face of
Meaninglessness.

The fourth *Vital* but too often missing *Life Saving Signal*
On the long road to true *Love* and long lasting *Intimacy*
You need to know
Is
Your ever-increasing and never-ending striving
To know why and how to be open and receptive to:
**Ultimate Meaning* or *Super-Meaning*
or
Meaning as Divine Design.

Dear spouses,
The best would be loving spouses among you
May not know why and how
To enjoy and share true and long lasting:
**love for each other,*
**peace with each other,*
**intimacy with each other*
When one or both of you
Face the faceless face of
Meaninglessness.

Imagine the day-to-day life's unbearable monotony
In a marriage where there is no forgiveness, no healing,
No wholeness, no honesty, no integrity, no humility,
No true and long lasting:
**love for each other,*
**peace with each other,*
**intimacy with each other.*

Ultimate meaning or Super-meaning
or Meaning as Divine Design
Is
What you need first if you are
To know why and how
To integrate and transcend *Meaning* as simple:
**social construct,*
**personal construct,*
**dialogical construct between social and personal construct.*

Their own Words

Ancient Greek philosopher,
Plato said:

Man is a being
in search for meaning.

Summary of the Chapter

Dear Spouses,
It is very difficult or even impossible
To have the will and skills and wisdom
You need
To love with true and long lasting *Love,*
To be loved with true and long lasting *Love,*
Enjoy and share true and long lasting *Peace*
With each other,
Enjoy and share true and long lasting *Intimacy*
With each other
When one or both of you face the face face
Of what neurologist, psychiatrist, and logotherapist
Viktor Emil Frankl calls:
The frustrated will to meaning…
Dear spouses, the *Meaning* of life,
The *Meaning* of your own life
Are some of your lifelong deepest needs.
The world most powerful powers,
The world tallest towers
Cannot compensate for your lack
Of true and long lasting:
**love for each other,*
**peace with each other,*
**intimacy with each other.*

Dear spouses, are you willing to fight with all your might to know why and how to prevent or *confront* and *overcome* what Viktor E. Frankl, calls:

- ★ *the existential vacuum?*
- ★ *the existential frustration?*
- ★ *the frustrated will to meaning, to power, to money, and to pleasure?*

If *Yes* is your answer, you then need also to know why and how to *transcend* your natural and normal but often limiting and misleading:

- ★ *meaning* as a simple *social construct,*
- ★ *meaning as a simple personal construct,*
- ★ *meaning as a simple dialogical encounter between social and personal constructs.*

To enjoy and share true and long lasting *meaning,* you need to know why and how to be open and receptive to:

- ★ *ultimate meaning,*
- ★ *or super-meaning,*
- ★ *or meaning as divine design.*

Ultimate Meaning or Super-Meaning
or Meaning as Divine Design
Is
Your pathway to a more meaningful life
In a more meaningful world for every thinking soul.

Your openness and receptivity to
Ultimate Meaning
Is
One of your best ways to a more peaceful life
In a more peaceful world for every thinking soul.

To enjoy and share true and long lasting:
★*love for each other,*

**peace with each other,*
**intimacy with each other,*
You need to know why and how
To act, interact and react, at the same time, as:
**social human beings,*
**individuals human beings,*
**spiritual beings.*

Their Own Words

Os Guinness, author of *Long Journey HOME: A Guide To Your Search For The Meaning Of Life,* starts his book with the following remark of a successful businessman:

I am at a point in my life where I realize
that there has to be something more.
Like many of my friends around here,
I've learned a lesson
I wish I'd known when I started out.
Having it all just isn't enough.
There is a limit to the success worth counting
and the toys worth accumulating.
Business school never gave me a calculus
for assessing the deeper things of life.

Dear spouses, *ultimate meaning or super-meaning or meaning as the divine design* is one of the deeper things in your life.

You need to be in touch with and deeply touched by *the deeper things* in your life if you are to know why and how to enjoy and share:

- *true love, aliveness, a meaningful life in a meaningful world...*
- *forgiveness, healing, wholeness, ultimate meaning...*
- *the emergence of your own and each other's true Self...*

The role and importance of *the deeper things in life* are depicted by the following life learning and life-changing question the Scriptures ask for anyone with a thinking soul:

What do you have when you gain the whole world but lose your own soul?

For all true believers, the obvious answer is *Nothing.*

The world great religious and spiritual traditions and collective wisdom tell us that:

- ★ *we each and all are created at God-image,*
- ★ *we each and all are created at God-likeness,*
- ★ *God is all-loving, all-knowing, all-powerful.*

That means that every loving spouse has all the potentialities to enjoy and share true and long lasting:

- ★ *love for each other,*
- ★ *peace with each other,*
- ★ *intimacy with each other.*

Even when you face life's inevitable failures, lack, temporary setbacks, betrayal, bitter divorce... you still have all the potentialities you need to:

- ★ *love truly and live fully alive,*
- ★ *forgive, forget, heal and be whole,*
- ★ *move on with your life even after betrayal and bitter divorce.*

The Problem

The fourth major barrier to true *Love* and long lasting *Peace* and *Intimacy* every loving spouse needs to know is why and how to:

- ★ *avoid the limiting and misleading Meaninglessness,*
- ★ *or confront the limiting and misleading Meaninglessness,*
- ★ *and overcome* the limiting and misleading *Meaninglessness.*

Meaninglessness is due to the *Soma/Spirit/Split.*

You live in two distinct yet intimately interconnected worlds.

You live, at the same time, in a material world and in a spiritual world.

When you try to live as if your whole world were merely material, you compromise your openness and receptivity to:

- ★ *ultimate meaning,*
- ★ *or super-meaning,*
- ★ *or meaning as divine design.*

Ultimate meaning or meaning as divine design involves but encompasses *meaning* as a simple:

- ★ *social construct,*
- ★ *personal construct,*
- ★ *dialogical encounter between social and personal construct.*

Dear spouses, you need to be touched by *ultimate meaning* if you are to know why and how to understand, enjoy, share and celebrate:

- ★ *the meaning of life,*
- ★ *the meaning of your own life,*
- ★ *the meaning of your own life destiny.*

When you have no meaning, no hope, no joy, no purpose, and no worthy cause, that is a wide-open door to all kinds of addictions in your day-to-day life.

Any addiction of any kind can be a smooth road to:

- ★ *the existential vacuum,*
- ★ *the existential frustration,*
- ★ *the frustrated will to meaning, to power, to money, to pleasure.*

To lose the meaning of life and the meaning of your own life is to lose the will and skills and wisdom you need to know why and how to:

- *get back up when you are down...*
- *fight back against your life's inevitable challenges...*
- *survive and thrive even after bitter divorce...*

For instance, the prisoners of the Nazi's concentration camp at *Auschwitz, Poland,* died daily due to their harsh conditions of existence and the loss of:

- *the meaning of their life,*
- *the meaning of their own life,*
- *any hope, purpose, joy, happiness...*

Their own Story

World neurologist, psychiatrist, and logo-
therapist, Viktor Emil Frankl,
was one of the survivors of one of the Nazi's
deadliest Concentrations Camps.

Viktor E. Frankl survived where thousands
of men, women, and children died.

When asked how he managed to survive
where so many people died
on a daily basis, he simply replied:

I knew that my attitude was my own choice.
I could choose to despair.
I could choose to be hopeful.
I choose to be hopeful.

But to be hopeful, he needed someone he loves truly
or something he was truly passionate about.

He found both in his wife, the love of his
life, and in his professional life
mostly dedicated to *Man Search for Meaning...*

His focus on something meaningful to his life and
on someone, he loves dearly kept him alive.

Concerning his wife, for instance, he was focused on her hands,
he wanted to hold one more time. He was focused on her eyes,
he wanted to look into one more time.
He was focused on being able
to embrace her one more time.

His passion for his profession and the
love of his wife kept him alive
till the allied forces arrived to liberate
Auschwitz from the Nazi's stronghold.

Lifelessness

Meaninglessness is a tween sister to *lifelessness.*

Their own Words

The myth of Sisyphus, by French writer Albert
Camus, is a typical example
where the same thing may mean different things to different people.

After having betrayed some divine secrets, Sysiphus was condemned to roll a stone at the top of a hill for the rest of his life.

Every time he pushed the stone at the top of the hill, the stone rolled right back to the bottom of the hill.

For some thinkers, Sysiphus's labor was arduous, repetitious, painful, and meaningless. He was going nowhere. He was doing nothing new, and nothing fresh. His situation was pointless. His labor was endless.

There was no light at the endless tunnel of Sysiphus's meaningless life. He was living a lifeless life. He was dead while seemingly alive.

For other thinkers, there were still some resting moments in Sysiphus's restless life. To them, Sysiphus could have some resting moments every time on his way back to the bottom of the hill to retrieve the stone.

As Albert Camus himself said:

"The struggle toward the summit itself suffices to fulfill a man's heart."

Dear spouses, you may:

- ★ *face your own disowned and wounded innocent Inner Child,*
- ★ *face the deep and unfathomable Inner Void within one or both of you,*
- ★ *feel the ineffable and unbearable Pain of Inner Emptiness within one or both of you,*
- ★ *you may still have all the potentialities you need to stand up and fight back.*

Start fighting back with all your might here and now.

The Solution

The *Solution* to the limiting and misleading *Meaninglessness* is to inspire each other to know why and how to:

- ★ *confront the limited Soma/Spirit/Split,*
- ★ *overcome the limiting Soma/Spirit/Split,*
- ★ *transcend the misleading Soma/Spirit/Spirit.*

The fundamental question in philosophy is to know if the world is merely *Material* or solely *Spiritual.*

Some of the world's great philosophers see the world as material. Other still world great philosophers see the world as spiritual.

Who is right and who is wrong?

Can both sides be both right and wrong at the same time?

Dear spouses, you have two fundamental needs. You have, at the same time, material needs and spiritual needs.

These two fundamental needs are two equally important needs.

You need to know why and how to satisfy both needs, ideally, at the same time.

For instance, if you try to satisfy your material need at the detriment of your spiritual need, you run the risk of facing the faceless face of:

- ★ *the existential vacuum,*
- ★ *the existential frustration,*
- ★ *the frustrated will to meaning, to power, to money, to pleasure at its lowest level.*

You need to know why and how to enjoy and share your material need and your spiritual need, at the same time, if you are to know why and how to enjoy and share:

- ★ *Ultimate Meaning,*
- ★ *or Super-Meaning,*
- ★ *or Meaning as Divine Design.*

You may know why and how to enjoy and share *Ultimate Meaning* anytime, anywhere, and under almost any life circumstance by and through your:

- ★ *true and long lasting love,*
- ★ *strong belief systems,*
- ★ *solid worldviews.*

The Power of your True and Long Lasting Love

Their own Words

In reflecting on his life learning experiences
in the Nazi's concentration Camps, Viktor E. Frankl said:

We who live in concentration camps can remember the men who walked through the hut comforting others and giving away their last piece of bread. They may have been few in numbers, but they offer sufficient proof that everything can be taken away from a man but one thing: the last of human freedom… to choose one's attitude in any given set of circumstances...

True and long-lasting love can be enjoyed and shared even in the face of imminent death.

True love is the source, the essence, and the quintessence of man' 4 deepest educational needs for:

- ★ *belonging,*
- ★ *relative independence,*
- ★ *dialogical encounter between belonging and relative independence,*
- ★ *self-navigation.*

For some spiritual gurus, we each and all are spiritually meant to:

- ★ *love all those who love us,*
- ★ *love even all those who hate us,*
- ★ *forgive all those who hurt us.*

Dear spouses, the quality of your education in general and the quality of the parenting style you've been through in particular, determine a great deal of your ability to:

- ★ *love your own self with Healthy Self-Love,*
- ★ *love each other with Spiritual Love,*
- ★ *love each other with Unconditional Love.*

The Power of your Belief Systems and Worldviews

Wake up during the wee hours of the night. Sit or standstill. Listen to the deep silence. Pray or meditate.

Enjoy and share the ineffable beauty, bounty, melody, and harmony of the world deep within you and all around you.

Lean on, learn from and build upon the positive side of your day-to-day life.

When you succeed, you may find life-changing ideas about why and how so many different people from so many different walks of life from so many different social and cultural backgrounds go faithfully to *church, the mosque, the synagogue, the temple, or any other shrine.*

Forget for a while your past fears, failures, lacks, and temporary setbacks. Forget for a while your innate talent, academic achievements, titles…

Plunge deep into the most sensitive strings of your innermost being. Ask yourself the following 4 life learning and life-changing questions:

- ★ *is meaning in my daily life solely a social construct?*
- ★ *is meaning in my daily life merely a personal construct?*

- *is meaning in my daily life a social and a personal construct?*
- *is meaning in my daily life beyond any limiting social and personal construct?*

Your answers to these questions may help you realize that *meaning* in your daily life is at the same time:

- *a social construct,*
- *a personal construct,*
- *a dialogical encounter between social and personal construct,*
- *a divine/spiritual construct beyond any limiting and misleading human construct.*

That is why divine love, divine grace, divine guidance is what you need first and the most if you are to know why and how to enjoy and share true and long lasting:

- *healthy self-love, inner peace so vital to peace with each other,*
- *love for each other,*
- *peace and intimacy with each other.*

Dear spouses, ask yourself the following life learning and life-changing questions:

- *who am I?*
- *where do I come from?*
- *where am I heading to?*

Once you do, you may understand Carl G. Jung's statement when he said:

- *modern man's biggest problem is not a personality problem,*
- *modern man's biggest problem is a religious or a spiritual problem.*

That is why you need to inspire each other to know why and how to be fully aware and deeply convinced that there is always:

- *something more,*
- *something bigger,*
- *something better.*

CHAPTER 5

Overcome Mindlessness

Step 5

Dear spouses, ***Step 5*** *to true Love and long lasting Peace*
and *Intimacy every loving spouse needs to know is why and*
how to tap into the Powerful life-giving and life animating
Power of Mindfulness.

Dear spouses,
To be mindful is to know why and how to:
★read between the lines,
★learn how to unlearn,
★see more than eye can see.

To be mindful is to know why and how
To *enjoy and share and celebrate:*
★love instead of hatred,
★peace instead of war,
★harmony instead of animosity.

To be mindful is to know why and how
To confront constructively life inevitable *Conflicts.*
To be mindful is to know why and how to enjoy and share
All the will and skills and wisdom you need to:
★read each other as you read a romance novel,
★feel each other's deep feelings,
★understand each other's deep but often hidden needs.

If you are to enjoy and share true and long lasting:
★love for each other,

★peace with each other,
★intimacy with each other
You need to know why and how to:
★see in each other more than your naked eyes can see,
★hear each other's unheard cry for Ultimate Meaning,
★understand each other's ultimate longings for *Inner Peace.*

Their own Words

Lewis M. Andrews, Ph.D., said:

In healing ourselves, we learn
that the greatest wisdom of all
lies not in listening to others but
in being true to our deepest selves.

Dear spouses,
The sixth *Vital* but often missing *Life Saving Signal*
On the long road to true *Love* and long lasting *Peace*
and Intimacy every loving spouse needs to know
Is
The powerful life-giving and life animating power of
MINDFULNESS.

You cannot enjoy and share true and long lasting:
★*love for each other,*
★*peace with each other,*
★*intimacy with each other*
When one or both of you face the faceless face of
MINDLESSNESS.

The fifth *Vital* but too often missing *Life Saving Signal*
On the long road to true *Love* and long lasting *Peace and*
Intimacy you need to know
Is
Your ever-increasing and never-ending striving
To know why and how to:
★*love all those who love you,*
★*love all those who hate you,*
★*forgive all those who hurt you.*

Lean on the positive side of your everyday life,
Learn from the positive side of your everyday life,
Build upon the positive side of your everyday life;
Be fully aware and deeply convinced
That only hurting people hurt other people.

Dear spouses,
The best would be loving spouses among you
May not know why and how
To enjoy and share true and long lasting:
**love for each other,*
**peace with each other,*
**intimacy with each other*
When one or both of you
Face the faceless face of
MEANINGLESSNESS.

The Unity, Balance, Harmony...
Between your *Outer World*
And your *Inner World*
Is
Your best way to:
**the best there is deep within you,*
**the best there is all around you,*
**the best there is within and all around both of you.*

Their own Words

Mindfulness guru, Harvard professor of psychology,
Ellen J. Langer said:

Most of what we learn from school, at home,
from television and from nonfiction books,
we may
mindlessly accept because it is given to us in an
unconditional form...
Most of what we know about the world,
about other people and about ourselves
is usually processed in the same way.

Summary of the Chapter

Dear Spouses,
It is very difficult or even impossible
To have the will and skills and wisdom
You need
To love with true and long lasting *Love,*
To be loved with true and long lasting *Love,*
To enjoy and share true and long lasting *Peace*
With each other,
To enjoy and share true and long lasting *Intimacy*
With each other
When one or both of you face the faceless face
Of ***Mindlessness.***
Mindlessness is a major barrier
To your marriage stability and harmony and happiness,
To your will and skills and wisdom
To read each other between the lines,
To see in each other more than eye can see,
To understand each other beyond the spoken words,
To attend to each other's deep hidden needs.

Dear spouses, are you willing to fight with all your might to know why and how to:

- ★ *read between the lines?*
- ★ *learn how to unlearn so that you could learn better?*
- ★ *confront constructively your life's inevitable Conflicts?*

If *Yes* is your answer, you then need also to know why and how to see:

- ★ *a message beneath every mess,*
- ★ *adversity as a great university,*
- ★ *a star beyond every scar.*

Dear spouses,
If you are to enjoy and share true and long lasting:
★*love for each other,*
★*peace with each other,*
★*intimacy with each other*
You need to know why and how to:
★*read each other as you read a romance novel,*
★*feel each other's deep feelings,*
★*understand each other's hidden needs.*

Their own Words

French writer, Anatole France, said:

A dog does not look at the blue azure sky
because there is nothing in it to eat.

But we, we are human beings.

We are the only *creatures* created in the image and likeness of our *Creator.*

Along with our material needs, we have other deep needs and ultimate longings.

We have our spiritual needs.

Dear spouses, as human and spiritual beings, you have both:

- ⋆ *material needs,*
- ⋆ *and spiritual needs.*

Your spiritual needs cannot be taught.

You spititual needs cannot be bought.

Your spiritual needs must be caught.

Your spiritual needs must be caught by and through your openness and receptivity to:

- ⋆ *the Larger than Life deep within you,*
- ⋆ *the Larger than Life all around you,*
- ⋆ *the Larger than Life between the best there is within and all around both of you.*

When your material needs are temporarily satisfied, you, as a loving couple, may be very delighted to hold hands and go for a long walk.

You may want to enjoy the ineffable beauty, bounty, melody, and harmony of the world around you.

You may contemplate:

- ⋆ *the blue azure sky,*
- ⋆ *the multicolored horizon during sunset,*
- ⋆ *the moonlight and the starry nights.*

As spiritual beings, you have deep needs and ultimate longings you canot:

- ⋆ *see,*
- ⋆ *touch,*

- ★ *trade with all the gold and diamond of the world.*

Your intangible and imponderable needs are as fundamental as your needs for:

- ★ *some fresh air to breath,*
- ★ *some healthy food to eat,*
- ★ *a roof, a room, and a safe place called home.*

Dear spouses, you may wonder why *there is more to your life than a mere living. You need a living conducive to a meaningful life. Indeed, a decent living does not necessarily guarantee a meaningful life.*

Your living is about your day-to-day struggle for material things and leisure and pleasure.

Your life is about your deepest needs and ultimate longings such as your true and long lasting longings for:

- ★ *a meaningful life,*
- ★ *a peaceful life,*
- ★ *purposeful life.*

Today, more than ever before, many people in general, many spouses in particular are living as if their whole world were merely about their material needs.

They act, interact and react as if their whole life were only about:

- ★ *matter and not spirit,*
- ★ *reason and not emotion,*
- ★ *logic and not intuition.*

Their own Words

Harvard professor of psychology, Ellen J. Langer, said:

We can change our school and our curricula and our standards for testing students and teachers.

We can increase parents and community involvement in the process of education and budget for education so that more students can be part of the computer age.
But none of these measures alone will make enough difference unless students are given the opportunity to learn mindfully.

Whether the learning is practical or theoretical,
whether it is personal or interpersonal,
whether the learning involves abstract concepts such as physics,
or concrete skills, such as how to play a sport,
the way the information is learned will determine
why, how, and when it is used.

The Problem

Dear spouses, the fifth major barrier to true *Love* and long lasting *Peace* and *Intimacy* every loving spouse needs to know is why and how to:

- ⋆ *avoid the limiting and misleading Mindlessness,*
- ⋆ *or confront the limiting and misleading Mindlessness,*
- ⋆ *and overcome the limiting and misleading Mindlessness.*

Mindlessness is due to the arbitrary *Split* between *Matter* and *Spirit,* known as *Soma/Spirit/Split.*

Dear spouses, you live in two distinct yet intimately interconnected worlds.

You live, at the same time, in a material world and in a spiritual world.

When you live as if your whole world were merely material, you undermine and compromise your openness and receptivity to your *Internal Learning World.*

Your *Internal Learning World* is what helps you know why and how to:

- ★ *read each other between the lines,*
- ★ *learn how to unlearn so that you could learn better,*
- ★ *see in each other more than your naked eyes can see.*

Your Mindfulness is a major effort to understand each other beyond your *Persona-mask.*

Carl G. Jung characterizes the natural and normal *Persona-mask* as simple:

- ★ *masquerade,*
- ★ *or facade,*
- ★ *or social wrapping.*

You are more than your social appearance.

Your social appearance or *Persona-mask* is far below who truly you are as a human and a spiritual being longing for healing, wholeness, and ultimate meaning.

Who you are on the *Inside* determines a great deal of the quality of your life and love and marriage.

For instance, if you lie to your own self, you may lie to anyone else including to your loving, caring, honest and humble spouse.

What lies deep within you defies your:

- ★ *reason,*
- ★ *logic,*
- ★ *statistics,*
- ★ *hard facts.*

If you are to enjoy and share a happy life and marriage, you need to know why and how to be true to each other's true *Self.*

Your true *Personality* is crucial to your ability to know why and how to:

- ★ *face constructively your life inevitable Uncertainties,*
- ★ *seek a balance between your external Authorities and your inner Autonomy,*
- ★ *harmonize the natural and normal pairs of your personal Inner Opposites.*

The Balance between your life's inevitable Conflicts is the best way to go in your struggle for a happy life and marriage.

The expression of your true and total *Personality* is, beyond your *Persona-mask,* what you need if you are to know why and how to enjoy and share true and long lasting:

- ★ *love for each other,*
- ★ *peace with each other,*
- ★ *intimacy with each other.*

The Solution

The *Solution* to *Mindlessness* is to inspire each other to know why and how to:

- ★ *confront the too limited Soma/Spirit/Split,*
- ★ *overcome the too limiting Soma/Spirit/Split,*
- ★ *get rid of the too misleading Soma/Spirit/Split.*

You have two equally important types of needs.

You have your material needs and you have your spiritual needs.

You need to know why and how to satisfy both needs, ideally, at the same time.

For instance, when you try to satisfy your material needs to the detriment of your spiritual needs, you may compromise your openness and receptivity to your *Internal Learning World.*

Your *Internal Learning World* is your built-in meaning-seeking and meaning-making machinery.

When you act and react as a whole, you are likely to know why and how to:

- ★ *accept, respect, and tolerate each other's natural difference,*
- ★ *read each other's deep and most hidden needs,*
- ★ *help each other treasure their own Priceless Inner Treasure that is in no other.*

Read Each Other Between The Lines

Your world is, at the same, as it is and as you each see it.

Sometimes, the higher your height, the lower your low.

Your spouse may be a good fighter.

Your spouse may be the main provider.

But your spouse may also be a nightmare to your innocent children's healthy growth.

Your spouse may be a major barrier to your innocent children:

- ★ *mental stability,*
- ★ *emotional balance,*
- ★ *healthy growth.*

Your children need a decent living conducive to a meaningful life.

A decent living without a meaningful life may push certain teens, adolescents, and young adults to rebel against their own parents and anyone else including their own self.

Dear spouses, think about how the parenting 3 massive mistakes may impact certain children:

- ★ *mental stability,*
- ★ *emotional balance,*
- ★ *healthy growth.*

A providing parent may hurt the children by and through one of the parenting 3 massive mistakes or:

- ★ *parents' way as almost the only way,*
- ★ *grown-up children' way as almost the only way,*
- ★ *parents and their teens...with no common way.*

Their own Story

On the one hand, rockstar Gyn L. Joplin said that:

★*on stage she makes love to 25,000 people.*

On the other hand, she sadly said that:

★*but then she goes home alone.*

She had name, fame, and fortune.

But she ends up ending her own life by heroin overdose at the young age of 27.

After her tragic death, one of her closest friends describes her as the most publicized homeless of the sixties. (re-adapted from Os Guinness's book, Long Journey HOME For The Search for The Meaning of Life.)

Learn How to Unlearn

Learn how to unlearn so that you could learn better.

Their own Story

Bertrand Russell was a well-known British mathematician and philosopher. He lived 98 years of a rational, calm, and successful professional life.

But his personal life was torn apart between his 4 wife (s) and many mistresses...

"...all the furies of Hell rage in his eyes...." said one of his many mistresses.

Bertrand Russell himself wrote to Otteline Morrel, one of his mistresses and said that:

"The root of the whole thing is loneliness...I have a kind of physical loneliness... which can be only relieved by a wife and children. Beyond, I have a very internal and terrible spiritual loneliness..."

As Os Guinness concluded, Bertrand Russell's longing for meaning, love, a home, a fulfilled life... speaks to us all.

A meaningful life is one of our lifelong deepest needs.

Some of the world's most successful people are enduring rather than enjoying their life.

They do not know why and how to enjoy and share true and long-lasting love and Ultimate Meaning.

To enjoy and share *Mindfulness*, you need to know why and how to see:

- ★ *a message beneath every mess,*
- ★ *adversity as a great university,*
- ★ *a star beyond every scar.*

See In Each Other More Eye Can See

Dear spouses,
Your *Outer World* is to your *Inner World,*
What the *Earth* is to the *Solar System,*
Just a tiny and tinny part of an infinite whole.

Our life is what our thoughts make it.
(Marcus Aurelius)

Dear spouses,
Narrow *mindedness* may lead your marriage
To one of the 3 following major issues:
★*my way is the only way,*
★*or my spouse's way is the only way,*
★*or my spouse and I have no common way.*

To *prevent or confront and overcome* narrow mindedness
Is to inspire each other to know why and how
To satisfy, ideally, at the same time,
your 4 deepest needs for:
★*Belonging,*
★*relative Independence,*
★*Dialogical Encounter,*
★*Self-navigation.*

CHAPTER 6
Overcome Shortsightedness

Step 6

Dear spouses, ***Step 6*** *to true Love and long lasting Peace*
and Intimacy every loving spouse needs to know is why and
how to:
★read each other as you read a romance novel,
★see in each other more than your naked eyes can see,
★inspire each other to bring out and share their own best.

Dear spouses,
The world great religious and spiritual traditions,
The world great collective wisdom,
The world great depth psychologists, psychoanalysts...
Tell us that there is always *something more and bigger and better.*
They also tell us that we each and all are divinely/spiritually
Meant to grow, develop and prosper including from the inside out.

Dear spouses,
You have two distinct learning worlds,
You have an external learning world,
You have an internal learning world.
Compared to your *Inner World, your Outer World*
Is
What the *Earth* is to the *Solar System*,
Just a tiny and tinny part of a larger whole.

Your *Inner World* is vital to the full expression
Of the deeper things in your life;
You need to know why and how

To be in touch with and deeply touched by
Each other's *Inner World,* so vital to your ability to:
★*read each other as you read a romance novel,*
★*feel each other's deep feelings,*
★*understand each other's hidden needs.*

The *why* you give what you give,
The *way* you give what you give,
The motifs behind
The *why* and the *way* you give what you give
Are all more important than *what you give.*

Their own Words

The author of *The Little Prince,*
Antoine de Saint-Exupéry, said:

What is essential in life cannot be seen
by the naked eye, what is essential in life
can only be seen by the heart.

Dear spouses,
The sixth *Vital* but too often missing *Life Saving Signal*
On the long road to true *Love* and long lasting
Peace and Intimacy
Every loving spouse needs to know
Is
The powerful life-giving and animating power
Of knowing why and how
To be in touch with and deeply touched by
THE LARGER THAN LIFE
Deep within and all around both of you.

You cannot enjoy and share true and long lasting:
**love for each other,*
**peace with each other,*
**intimacy with each other*
When one or both of you face the faceless face
Of the limiting and misleading
SHORTSIGHTEDNESS.

You live in two distinct yet intimately interconnected worlds,
You live in a material world,
You live in a spiritual world,
When you try to live as if your whole world
Were merely material,

You undermine and compromise your ability to:

★read each other as you read a romance novel,

★hear each other beyond your spoken words,

★see in each other more than your naked eyes can see.

Dear spouses,
The best would be loving spouses among you
May not know why and how
To enjoy and share true and long lasting:
⋆*love for each other,*
⋆*peace with each other,*
⋆*intimacy with each other*
As long as one or both of you
Do not know *why* and *how*
To see in each other
More than your naked eyes can see.

If you are to enjoy and share
Your will and skills and wisdom to:
⋆*read between the lines,*
⋆*hear beyond your spoken words,*
⋆*see more than eye can see,*
You need to know why and how
To navigate smoothly between:
⋆*your reason and your emotion,*
⋆*your logic and your intuition,*
⋆*your Persona-mask and your true Personality.*

Their own Words

French mathematician,
Henry Poincare said:

Pure logic is a tautology.
We discover with intuition.
We prove with logic.

Summary of the Chapter

Dear Spouses,
It is very difficult or even impossible
To have the will and skills and wisdom
You need
To love with true and long lasting *Love,*
To be loved with true and long lasting *Love,*
To enjoy and share true and long lasting *Peace*
With each other,
To enjoy and share true and long lasting *Intimacy*
With each other
When one of both of you face the faceless face
Of ***Shortsightedness***
With its too often mental blindness.
Your outer world is to your inner world
What planet *Earth* is the *Solar System*,
Just a tiny and tinny part of an infinite whole.
Your *eyesight* relies on and learns from and builds upon
What you can see and touch and rationalize
An explain and manipulate.
Your *mindsight* relies on and learns from
And builds upon
The powerful life-giving power,
Deep within you and all around you,

The powerful life animating power
Deep within you and all around you.
Your *mindsight* requires you
To be in touch with,
To be deeply touched by
The *Larger* than *Life* deep within both of you,
The *Larger* than *Life* all around both of you,
The *Larger* than *Life* in between the best there is
Deep within you and all around both of you.

Dear spouses, are you willing to fight with all your might to know why and how to be in touch with and deeply touched by the *Vital* ineffable something:

- ★ *more deep within you and all around both of you?*
- ★ *bigger deep within you and all around both of you?*
- ★ *better deep within you and all around both of you?*

If *Yes* is your answer, you then need also to know why and how to:

- ★ *see in each other more than your naked eyes can see,*
- ★ *hear each other beyond your spoken words,*
- ★ *understand each other beyond your rational mind.*

The ineffable *something more and bigger and better* lies, often dormant, deep within and all around both of you.

Dig it deep from the *"Inside Out."*

Go beyond your reasoning but often limiting and misleading rational mind.

Try to know why and how to enjoy and share *the ineffable something more and something bigger and something bette*r deep within and all around both of you.

To succeed, you need to know why and how to learn, at the same time, from your *External Learning World* and your *Internal Learning World*.

Use the *"Outside In"* to awaken your *Internal Learning World.*

Use your *Internal Learning World* to add meaning to your *External Learning World.*

Open your *heart and soul and spirit* to each other's heart, soul, and spirit.

Refuse to hide to each other your personal weaknesses such as your:

- ★ *subjectivity,*
- ★ *naivety,*
- ★ *vulnerability.*

Strive to be *One* with one another without losing your personal identity.

One of your best ways to be true to your own self is to have nothing to hide from each other.

When you are true to the true "you," you are likely to be true to each other's true *Self.*

When you are true to each other's true *Self,* it will be easier for both of you to:

- ★ *accept and respect and tolerate your natural difference,*
- ★ *forgive each other and forget and heal and be whole,*
- ★ *share a peaceful marriage in a peaceful environment.*

Listen to each other's loud but too often unheard cry for true and long lasting:

- ★ *love for each other,*
- ★ *peace with each other,*
- ★ *intimacy with each other.*

Learn why and how to see each other more than your naked *eyes* can see.

Learn why and how to find new and better ways of helping each other to:

- ★ *awaken their own Inner Splendor that is in no other,*
- ★ *treasure their own Priceless Inner Treasure that is in no other,*
- ★ *sing out loud their own favorite Love Song that has never been sung before.*

That is one of the first and the best gifts you can ever give to each other.

One of the greatest gifts you can give to each other is to know why and how to inspire them to be in touch with and deeply touched by:

- ★ *the best there is within them,*
- ★ *the best there all around them,*
- ★ *the best there is between their Inner World and their Outer World.*

For instance, one of the best and yet the most neglected gifts you can give to each other is to inspire them to know why and how to:

- ★ *awaken the positive side of their own Sleeping Giant that is in no other,*
- ★ *treasure their own Priceless Inner Treasure that is in no other,*
- ★ *sing their own most favorite Love Song that is in no other.*

Try to inspire each other to know why and how to:

- ★ *live fully alive,*
- ★ *forgive and forget,*
- ★ *heal and be whole...*

Wholeness is your pathway to the *Larger than Life*:

- ★ *deep within every one of you,*
- ★ *all around every one of you,*
- ★ *in between the best there is within and all around both of you.*

As human and spiritual beings, we are the only *creatures* created in the image and likeness of our *Creator.*

After having temporarily met our basic material needs, we often feel delighted by the ineffable beauty of:

- ★ *the blue azure sky,*
- ★ *the sunset during a sunny day,*
- ★ *the moonlight and the starry nights.*

Their own Words

In his book, *In Tune with the Infinite*, world bestselling author, Ralph Waldo Trine, said:

There is a divine sequence running throughout the universe.

Within and above and below, the human will...
works the divine will.

To come into harmony with it and thereby with all the higher laws and forces...is to come into the chain of this wonderful sequence.

This is the secret of all success.

This is to come into the possession of unknown riches,
into the realization of undreamed-of powers.

The Problem

Dear spouses, the sixth major barrier to true *Love* and long lasting *Peace* and *Intimacy* every loving spouse needs to know is why and how to:

- ★ *avoid the limiting and misleading Shortsightedness,*
- ★ *or confront the limiting and misleading Shortsightedness,*
- ★ *and overcome the limiting and misleading Shortsidness.*

Shortsightedness is due to the arbitrary *Soma/Spirit/Split. Shortsightedness* is a major barrier to your openness and receptivity to the *Larger than Life*:

- ★ *deep within both of you,*
- ★ *all around both of you,*
- ★ *in between the best there is within and all around both of you.*

If you are not in touch with and deeply touched by the *Larger* than *Life,* you undermine your openness and receptivity to:

- *ultimate meaning,*
- *or super meaning,*
- *or meaning as divine design.*

Shortsightedness is a major barrier to your will and skills and wisdom to know why and how to inspire each other to:

- *awaken the positive side of their own Sleeping Giant within that is in no other,*
- *treasure their own Priceless Inner Treasure that is in no other,*
- *share their own most favorite Love Song that is in no other.*

The world we live in is more than:

- *we can see,*
- *we can touch,*
- *we can comprehend.*

As a French philosopher,
Michel de Montaigne, said:

Man is a whole,
if you mutilate one part,
you destroy the whole.

Like Michel de Montaigne's man, the world too is a whole. If we split it in matter versus spirit, we may destroy it.

Dear spouses,
Shortsightedness is too limited,
Shortsightedness is too limiting,
Shortsightedness is too misleading,
Shortsightedness
Is
A too limited and limiting and misleading road

To your will and skills and wisdom to:
★read each other between the lines,
★hear each other beyond your spoken words,
★understand each other beyond your Persona-mask.

The Solution

The *Solution to Shortsightedness* is to know why and how to inspire each other to *transcend* the too limiting and too misleading *Soma/Spirit/Split*.

Remember the *Scriptures'* life learning and life-changing question:

What do you have when you gain the whole world but lose your own soul?

For all true believers, the obvious answer is *Nothing*.

Learn why and how to enjoy and share, at the same time, your material needs and your spiritual needs.

To succeed, be in touch with and deeply touched by the *Larger than Life*:

- ★ *deep within both of you,*
- ★ *all around both of you,*
- ★ *in between the best there is within and all around both of you.*

Enjoy and share the *Larger than Life* within and around both of you by and through:

- ★ *true love,*
- ★ *strong belief systems and solid worldviews,*
- ★ *forgiveness, healing, wholeness, and your true Self.*

See in Each Other More than Eye Can See

One of the most memorable gifts you can give to each other is to inspire them to know why and how to:

- ★ *identify their own true identity,*
- ★ *be true to their own true identity,*
- ★ *become who truly they are meant to be.*

Identify who truly you are. Inspire each other to:

- ★ *identify what they want most out of their life,*
- ★ *identify what they are most good at,*
- ★ *re-align what they are most good at to what they want most out of their life.*

Dear spouses,
If you are to enjoy and share true and long lasting:
★*love for each other,*
★*peace with each other,*
★*intimacy with each other*
You need to know why and how to:
★*read each other between the lines,*
★*hear each other beyond your spoken words,*
★*see in each other more than your naked eyes can see.*

Your world is at the same time as it is and as you each see it.
What is decent for one of you may be indecent for the other,
What is good for one of you may be bad for the other.
In some degree, you may see differently the same thing,
What is natural and normal and necessary for one
Maybe awkward for the other.
Be open and receptive to each other:
★*inner splendor,*
★*natural gift,*
★*dominant talent.*

In life and in love and in marriage, start here and now
Your ever-increasing and never-ending struggle
To know why and how to:
★play on a common ground, your marriage ideal playground,
★win the win-win game of life, your marriage ideal winning style,
★stay in the middle, your marriage ideal pathway to freedom.

When only one of you wins,
You both lose,
When you both lose,
It may be a nightmare for:
★the whole family,
★the whole neighborhood.

PART III

How to Transcend the 3 Types of Love that Prevent Would be Loving Spouses from Knowing Why and How to Love Each Other with True Love and Long-Lasting Peace and Intimacy?

Getting in touch with your heart is like
plugging into that universal consciousness or spirit.
Your heart is a little computer that plugs into the cosmic
computer where everything is inseparably one.
(Deepack Chopra. spiritual guru)

Dear spouses,

The 3 natural and normal and necessary
But too often too limiting and misleading
Types of love that prevent would-be loving spouses
From knowing why and how
To enjoy and share true and long lasting:
★*love for each other,*
★*peace with each other,*
★*intimacy with each other*
are
What Isador Schneider, in his book,
The World of Love, calls:
★*Need-Love,*
★*Gift-Love,*
★*Mature Love.*

Need-love, Gift-love, and Mature love are natural and normal
But too often too limiting and misleading types of love.
If you are to enjoy and share true and long lasting:
★*love for each other,*
★*peace with each other,*
★*intimacy with each other*
You need to know why and how to *Transcend:*
★ *Need-love,*
★*Gift-love,*
★*Mature love.*

The first biggest massive mistake in love and in marriage
Is
To fall in love with and marry each other's
Simple *Persona-mask*
At the detriment of each other's
True and total *Personality.*

Dear spouses,
Your deep need and ultimate longing
For true and long lasting:
**love for each other,*
**peace with each other,*
**intimacy with each other*
Involve but encompasse
Your natural and normal and necessary
But often limiting and misleading:
**Need-love,*
**Gift-love,*
**Mature love.*

Your deep need and ultimate longing
For true and long lasting:
**love for each other,*
**peace with each other,*
**intimacy with each other*
Require each other's will and skills and wisdom
To know why and how to enjoy and share more than:
**Need-love,*
**Gift-love,*
**Mature love.*

Your true *Love* and long lasting
Peace and *Intimacy* for each other
Require:
**healthy self-love,*
**divine/spiritual love,*
**unconditional love.*

CHAPTER 7

Transcend Need-Love

Step 7

Dear spouses, ***Step 7*** *to true Love and long lasting Peace and Intimacy every loving spouse needs to know is why and how to enjoy and share more than the natural and normal but too often too limited and limiting and misleading* ***Need-Love.***

Dear spouses,
Need-love is natural and normal and necessary,
But *Need-love* is often limited and a misleading
Road to true and long lasting:
**love for each other,*
**peace with each other,*
**intimacy with each other.*

In his book, *The World of Love*, Isadore Schneider
Characterizes *Need-love*
When one's personal needs and interests and comfort
Are made predominant and more important
Than the other's personal needs and interests and comfort.

Need-love lovers are the innocent victims
Of the parenting second massive mistake
Or teens, adolescents, and young adults' way as almost the only way,
Or what psychologist of *Artistic Creativity*, Otto Rank,
Calls *the Fear of Death.*
Need-love lovers want to initiate it all,
They want to dominate and control it all
While in life and in love and in marriage,

The *middle* is the ideal pathway to *wisdom,*
The common ground is the ideal playground,
The *win-win* is marriage stability's ideal winning style.

Spouses who are victims of *the Fear of Death*
See their own way as the only way.
Imagine a marriage where one spouse decides,
Commands and controls it all,
While the other spouse has to endure it all
Without knowing why and how to enjoy and share
His/her two first deepest and equally important needs
For *Belonging* and for relative *Independence.*

Their own Words

Bill Russel said:

To love someone is nothing,
To be loved by someone is something,
To love someone who loves you, that is everything.

Dear spouses,
The seventh *Vital* but too often missing *Life Saving Signal*
On the long road to true love and long lasting peace and intimacy
Every loving spouse needs to know
Is
To know why and how to enjoy and share more than
NEED-LOVE.

You cannot enjoy and share true and long lasting:
**love for each other,*
**peace with each other,*
**intimacy with each other*
When one or both of you face the faceless face
Of the natural and normal and necessary
But too often limited, limiting, and misleading
NEED-LOVE.

The seventh *Vital* but too often missing *Life Saving Signal*
On the long road to true *Love* and long lasting *Peace and Intimacy*
You need to know
Is
Your ever-increasing and never-ending striving
To know why and how
To meet and meltdown and be *One* with one another other
Without losing your personal *Identity.*

Dear spouses,
The best would be loving spouses among you
May not know why and how
To enjoy and share true and long lasting:
★*love for each other,*
★*peace with each other,*
★*intimacy with each other*
When one or both of you face the faceless face of:
★*the wounded innocent Inner Child within one or both of you,*
★*the deep and unfathomable Inner Void within one or both of you,*
★*the unbearable Pain of Inner Emptiness within one or both of you.*

If you are to enjoy and share true and long lasting:
★*love for each other,*
★*peace with each other,*
★*intimacy with each other,*
You must know why and how to:
★*prevent successfully,*
★*or confront constructively,*
★*and overcome definitively*
★*the wounded innocent Inner Child within one or both of you,*
★*the deep and unfathomable Inner Void within one or both of you,*
★*the unbearable Pain of Inner Emptiness within one of both of you.*

Their Own Words

Theologian, physician, and humanitarian,
Albert Schweitzer, said:

I don't know what your destiny will be, but one thing
I do know:
the only ones among you who will be really happy
are those who have sought and found how to serve.
As the sun makes the ice melt, kindness causes
misunderstanding, mistrust, and hostility evaporate.

Summary of the Chapter

Dear Spouses,
It is very difficult or even impossible
To have the will and skills and wisdom
You need
To love with true and long lasting *Love,*
To be loved with true and long lasting *Love,*
To enjoy and share true and long lasting *Peace*
With each other,
To enjoy and share true and long lasting *Intimacy*
With each other
When one or both of you face the faceless face
Of the natural and normal
But too often too limited, too limiting, and too misleading
Need-Love.
In life, in love, in marriage…
There are things the world's richest
Gold and diamond mines cannot buy.
True love, inner peace so vital peace with each other,
True and long lasting intimacy with each other
Will never be for sale.

In life, in love, in marriage...
The common ground is marriage's playground,
The win-win is marriage's winning style,
The middle is marriage's pathway to happiness.
Imagine a marriage when one spouse
Has to dominate and dictate and control it all,
While the other spouse
Has to leave or to endure it all...

Dear spouses, are you willing to fight with all your might to know why and how to:

- ★ *welcome the emergence of your own true Self,*
- ★ *welcome the emergence of each other's true Self,*
- ★ *enjoy and share and celebrate more than Need-love?*

If *Yes* is your answer, you then need also to know why and how to *transcend* your natural and normal but often limiting and misleading:

- ★ *socially induced self,*
- ★ *self-imposed self,*
- ★ *dialogical encounter induced self.*

To succeed, you need to know why and how to:

- ★ *enjoy the life-giving and life animating power of your own true Self,*
- ★ *share the life-giving and animating power of each other's true Self,*
- ★ *celebrate the spiritual guidance of your true, transcendent, infinite Self.*

Dear spouses,
You cannot enjoy and share true and long lasting:
★*love for each other,*
★*peace with each other,*
★*intimacy with each other*
When you do not know why and how to be in touch with:
★*each other's true Self,*
★*each other's transcendent Self,*
★*each other's infinite Self.*

Need-love lovers are focused on what they can get from you. They are never interested in what you can get from them.

Need-love lovers' way has to be the only way. They give supremacy and priority to:

- ★ *their own personal needs,*
- ★ *their own personal interests,*
- ★ *their own personal comfort.*

Need-love lovers are after what they want.

They do not hesitate to spend time, energy, and resources to get what they want.

But once they get what they want, they are often gone for good.

Butterflies like, they are on their endless quest for new exotic and freshly blossom flowers.

French novelist, Marcel Proust,
was likely talking about *Need-love lovers' loving style* when he said:

The woman I love today
will not be the same woman
I will love tomorrow,
I myself will be
another man by then.

Their own Words

In their book, *The Art of Marriage Maintenance*,
Sylvia J. Karasu, MD and T. Bryam Karasu, MD,
reported the confession of a *Need-love lover's* instability.

I am, I am trying to behave.
I don't know why, but I am always looking for women.

My wife is young and beautiful and very good in bed.

I cannot claim to be deprived of sex.

Nevertheless, even after a few hours of satisfactory sex,
I find myself eyeing other women.

I can't listen reasonably to any good looking woman because
I am constantly imagining what she could be like in bed.

I love my wife, my family; I don't want to do anything to harm them.
I would never leave them for another woman.

Nevertheless, I tell other women...that I might leave my wife
if that is what it takes to get them to sleep with me.

I even go as far as lying that my wife is having an affair with my best friend
and will soon be leaving me.

If anything I am the one who is trying to sleep with the wives of our friends.

I know, I know, this is going to get me in trouble one of these days.

Did I tell you we just hired a young associated, who has a pair
of legs, you wouldn't believe?

The other evening I offered her a ride. She jumped at the opportunity.
We didn't stop talking all the way.

She couldn't understand why my wife would even consider having sex
with another man and leave someone like me—intelligent, handsome, witty.

When we got to the parking lot...noticing how
unaffected I was with her flattery,
she resorted to a more convincing tactic. Oh my, oh my...?

The Problem

Dear spouses, the seventh major barrier to true *Love* and long lasting *Peace* and *Intimacy* every loving spouse needs to know is why and how to:

- ★ *prevent the natural and normal but limiting and misleading Need-love,*
- ★ *or confront the natural and normal but limiting and misleading Need-love.*
- ★ *and overcome the natural and normal but limiting and misleading Need-love.*

Need-love lovers' domineering attitude is due to:

- ★ *the parenting second massive mistake,*
- ★ *or what psychologist, Otto Rand, calls the Fear of Death,*
- ★ *or need-love lovers own instinctual tyranny.*

The parenting second massive mistake or teens, adolescents and young adults' way as almost the only way exposes certain children to what Otto Rank calls *the Fear of Death.*

According to the psychologist of *Artistic Creativity,* Otto Rank,
from the trauma of birth to the trauma of death,
people experience two types of fear:

★*the Fear of Life*
★*and the Fear of Death.*

Need-love lovers are the innocent victims of *the Fear of Death.*

Their Fear of Death experienced during their childhood may last a lifetime.

It may impact their love and marriage style.

The *Fear of Death* induces certain spouses to:

- ★ *self-centeredness,*
- ★ *self-fishness,*
- ★ *aggressiveness because their own way has to be the only way...*

Need-love lovers act and interact and react as if their way were the only way.

While in life and in love and in marriage, the *middle* is the ideal pathway to *wisdom*.

But, *Need-love lovers*' way has to be the only way.

Their domineering attitude can be so upsetting to their love partner.

Need-love lovers do not hesitate to dump you as soon as they know you.

Once they know you, you are no longer the one and the only chosen one.

They may use you and abuse you.

They may leave you and forget you as if they have never known you.

How heartbreaking it is to give your heart to someone who has no heart.

Your first reaction is not to complain or explain or cry and ask "why me, why me…"

It is not your fault. It is theirs. And there is little or nothing you can do about it.

All you need is to forgive and forget what they did to you and move on with your life.

Need-love lovers have been the innocent victims of the second parenting massive mistake long before they met you and got married to you.

That is why and how so many men and so many women have a hard time:

- ★ *understanding each other,*
- ★ *trusting each other,*
- ★ *getting along with each other.*

That is why and how so many promising marriages end up with:

- ★ *instabilities,*
- ★ *infidelities,*
- ★ *bitter divorces.*

Their own Words

In their book**,** *The Art of Marriage Maintenance*,
Sylvia R. Karasu, M.D and T. Bryam Karasu, M.D
reported the confession of an adulterous husband
of a domineering wife:

*...I have no sexual desire for her. I don't like being with her.
Isn't that an awful thing to say about one's wife?*

But it's true…

She is such a ball-buster.

She talks to me as if I was her child or her servant.

If I protest her bossy behavior, she gets even nastier and explains impatiently why she has no choice other than to be exact with me, because I always fail in my role as a man and as a husband, that I am irresponsible, inadequate, you name it...

Something happens to me when I am around her, I even mumble when I am around her....when I talk to her.

No one in the world can...when physically or psychologically impotent.

With Gween, I am like a superman.

She says she never had an orgasm...before she
met me and I have no problem
in having an erection with her...

I feel good just being with these women even with sex.

What would my wife say when she finds out that I am having
an affair with my secretary...

She wouldn't believe it...
"Him? He wouldn't even find his way to first base."

The Solution

The *Solution* to the *Need-love lovers'* domineering attitude is to inspire them to know why and how to enjoy and share the *Balance* between their need for:

- *Belonging and for relative Independence,*
- *others' Authority and their own inner Autonomy,*
- *others' Expectations and their personal Inclination.*

The *Solution* to the *Need-love lovers'* tyrannical marriage lifestyle is to inspire them to know why and how to:

- *unify their Fear of Death with their Fear of Life,*
- *balance their Fear of Death with their Fear of Life,*
- *harmonize their Fear of Death with their Fear of Life.*

In life and in love and in marriage, *the middle is the ideal pathway to wisdom.*

Wisdom is vital to your marriage stability.

The win-win marriage style is the smoothest road to *marriage stability and happiness.*

In life and in love and in marriage:

- ★ *the common ground is the ideal playground,*
- ★ *the win-win is marriage's ideal winning style,*
- ★ *the middle is marriage's ideal pathway to happiness.*

Need-love lovers' domineering marriage style is deeply rooted in their upbringing style.

The deep root cause of their domineering lifestyle comes from their upbringing unresolved issues.

They are often *One* with their bad behavior without knowing why and how to get rid of it.

It is not easy to convince *Need-love lovers* to get rid of their selfishness.

To overcome their domineering attitudes requires *deep soul searching and moral courage and effort and healthy self-criticism.*

But healthy self-criticism is incompatible with selfishness.

To enjoy and share a happy marriage, you must know why and how to navigate smoothly between your two first deepest and equally important needs for:

- ★ *belonging,*
- ★ *and for relative Independence.*

The satisfaction of your first deepest *Need for Belonging* may help you enjoy *Oneness* without full *Self-awareness.*

You may know why and how to be *One* with your loved ones and important others without losing your personal identity and inner autonomy.

The satisfaction of your second deepest and equally important *need for relative Independence* helps you enjoy your own *Uniqueness* without *Selfishness*.

Excellence in your Education happens when you know why and how to Harmonize your deep need for Togetherness and your deep need for Uniqueness.

To give more importance to one educational need at the detriment of the other is the first and one of the worst root causes of:

- ★ *all educational failures at all levels,*
- ★ *all violence, including domestic violence,*
- ★ *all man-made tragedies.*

If you are to enjoy and share a happy marriage, you must know why and how to:

- ★ *need more than the natural but too limiting and misleading Need-love,*
- ★ *require more than the natural but too limiting and misleading Need-love,*
- ★ *enjoy and share more than the natural but too limiting and misleading Need-love.*

In her book,
Me: Stories of My Life,
Katherine Hepburn said:

Love has nothing to do
with what you are expecting to get...
[Love has everything to do]
...with what you are expecting to give---
which is everything.

Dear spouses,
There is a place, an ineffable place,
Deep within each and every one
Of us all as a whole,
Where we each and all
Are spiritually meant to meet and meltdown
To be *One* with one another
Without losing our personal identity.

If we are to be *One* with one another
Without losing our personal identity,
We first need to know why and how
To be *One* with our own:
⋆*true Self,*
⋆*transcendent Self,*
⋆*infinite Self.*

CHAPTER 8

Transcend Gift-Love

Step 8

Dear spouses, ***Step 8*** *to true Love* and long lasting *Peace* and *Intimacy every loving spouse needs to know is why and how to transcend the natural and normal but too often too limiting and too misleading* ***Gift-love.***

Dear spouses,
Gift-love lovers are the innocent victims
Of the parenting first massive mistake,
Or parents and important others' way as almost the only way,
Or what psychologist of *Artistic Creativity*, Otto Rank,
Calls *the Fear of Life.*

The Fear of Life pushes certain teens, adolescents...
To go through life with what French anthropologist
Lucien Levy Bruhl calls *Participation Mystique.*
Mere participation mystique
Limits certain people to *Oneness* without *Self-awareness.*
Oneness without full *Self-awareness*
Is a smooth and a straight and a fast road
To *blind conformity, apathy, mediocrity...*

Gilf-love lovers are on the opposite side
Of *Need-Love lovers.*
Gift-love lovers see their love partners'
Personal needs, interests, and comfort
As predominant and more important
Than their own personal needs, interests, and comfort.

In life, in love, in marriage,
Gift-lover lovers
Are frequent innocent victims of abuse and betrayal
And domestic violence and bitter divorce.

Their own Words

Kute Blackson, a motivational speaker, said:

The most important resource isn't time, or oil, money, or gold;
it's love.
Without [love] we may have everything but life is nothing.

Dear spouses,
The eighth *Vital* but too often missing *Life Saving Signal*
On the long road to true *Love* and long lasting *Peace and Intimacy*
Every spouse needs to know
Is
Why and how to give and require more than
The often limiting and misleading
GIFT-LOVE.

You cannot enjoy and share true and long lasting:
⋆*love for each other,*
⋆*peace with each other,*
⋆*intimacy with each other*
When one or both of you face the faceless face
Of the natural and normal
But too often too limiting and misleading
GIFT-LOVE.

The eighth *Vital* but often missing *Life Saving Signal*
On the long road to true *Love* and long lasting *Peace* and *Intimacy*
You need to know
Is
Your ever-increasing and never-ending striving
To know why and how to:
⋆*read each other as you read a romance novel,*
⋆*feel each other's deep feelings,*
⋆*understand each other's hidden needs.*

Dear spouses,
The best would be loving spouses among you
May not know why and how
To enjoy and share true and long lasting:
**love for each other,*
**peace with each other,*
**intimacy with each other*
As long as one or both of you face the faceless face
Of the natural and normal and necessary
But too often limited, limiting, and misleading
GIFT-LOVE.

Compared to your *Inner World*, your *Outer World*
Is what the *Earth* is to the *Solar System,*
Just a tiny and tinny part of an infinite whole.
Your *Outer World*
Is
To your *Inner World*,
What a small and stagnant lake
Is
To a bottomless and a shoreless ocean,
Their difference is not in degree,
Their difference is in their true nature.

Their own Words

Ivan Panin said:

For every beauty, there is an eye
somewhere to see it.
For every truth, there is an ear
somewhere to hear it.
For every love, there is a heart
somewhere to receive it.

Summary of the Chapter

Dear Spouses,
It is very difficult or even impossible
To have the will and skills and wisdom
You need
To love with true and long lasting *Love,*
To be loved with true and long lasting *Love,*
To enjoy and share true and long lasting *Peace*
With each other,
To enjoy and share true and long lasting *Intimacy*
With each other
When one or both of you face the faceless face
Of the natural and normal but too often
Too limited and too limiting and too misleading
Gift-Love
In life, in love, in marriage...
The common ground is your marriage's happiness playground,
The win-win is your marriage's happiness winning style,
The middle is your marriage's happiness pathway to happiness.
Imagine a marriage when one spouse

Gives priority and more importance
To the needs, the interests, and the comfort
Of the other spouse at the very detriment
Of his/her own needs, interests, and comfort.

Dear spouses, are you willing to fight with all your might to know why and how to:

- ★ *give more than Gift-love?*
- ★ *require more than Gift-love?*
- ★ *enjoy and share more than Gift-love?*

If *Yes* is your answer, you then need also to know why and how to:

- ★ *love each other with true and long lasting Love,*
- ★ *enjoy and share true and long lasting Peace,*
- ★ *enjoy and share true and long-lasting Intimacy.*

You must be true to your own true *Self* if you are to know why and how to:

- ★ *give more than Gift-love to your spouse,*
- ★ *require more than Gift-love from your spouse,*
- ★ *enjoy and share more than Gift-love with each other.*

Gift-love is natural and normal and necessary.

But *Gift-love* alone is often a too limiting and too misleading type of love.

Loving spouses should know why and how to fight with all their might to:

- ★ *give each other more than Gift-love,*
- ★ *require from each other more than Gift-love,*
- ★ *enjoy and share with each other more than Gift-love.*

Dear spouses,
To love truly is to see
In each other more than eye can see.
To love truly is to hear
Each other beyond the spoken words.
To love truly is to inspire each other
To know why and how to enjoy and share:

★true and long lasting love,
★true and long lasting peace,
★true and long-lasting intimacy.

To love truly is to know why and how
To inspire each other to:
★awaken the positive side of their own Sleeping
Giant within that is in no other,
★treasure their own Priceless Inner Treasure that is in no other,
★share their own most favorite Love Song that is in no other.

If you are to enjoy and share true and long lasting:
★love for each other,
★peace with each other,
★intimacy with each other
You must know why and how to:
★see in each other more than your naked eyes can see,
★hear each other beyond your spoken words,
★enjoy and share the best there is within and all around both of you.

Gift-love is natural and normal and necessary. *Gift-love* is a social and historical necessity.

But *Gift-love* alone is often a limiting and misleading type of love.

Some of the world great religious and spiritual traditions and collective wisdom tell us that:

★ *we each and all are created at God-image,*
★ *we each and all are created at God-likeness,*
★ *God is all-loving, all-knowing, all-powerful.*

For all true believers that means that we each and all are divinely/ spiritually meant to be:

★ *all-loving,*

- ★ *all-knowing,*
- ★ *all-powerful.*

Dear spouses, divinely, spiritually, and psychologically, no one is meant to:

- ★ *demean and dominate you,*
- ★ *be demeaned and dominated by you,*
- ★ *be less than an important member of the same important family: the Human Family.*

To love each other with true *Love* and long lasting *Peace* and *Intimacy* is to inspire each other to:

- ★ *identify their own true identity,*
- ★ *be true to their own true identity,*
- ★ *become who truly they are meant to be.*

Dear spouses, you must know why and how to be true to your own true *Self* if you are to know why and how to:

- ★ *love each other with healthy self-love,*
- ★ *love each other with spiritual love,*
- ★ *love each other with unconditional love.*

The Problem

Dear spouses, the eighth major barrier to true *Love* and long lasting *Peace and Intimacy* every loving spouse need to know is why and how to:

- ★ *avoid the natural and normal but often limiting and misleading Gift-love,*
- ★ *transcend the natural and normal but often limiting and misleading Gift-love,*
- ★ *overcome the natural and normal but often limiting and misleading Gift-love.*

Gift-love lovers' blind conformity is due to:

- ★ *the parenting first massive mistake,*
- ★ *or parents and important others' way as almost the only way,*
- ★ *or what psychologist of Artistic Creativity, Otto Rank, calls the Fear of Life.*

We have already quoted
the psychologist of *Artistic Creativity,*
Otto Rank, saying that:

From the trauma of birth
to the trauma of death,
people experience two types of fear:
★the Fear of Life,
★and the Fear of Death.

The first fear or the Fear of Life exposes certain children to:

- ★ *mere participation mystique,*
- ★ *blind conformity,*
- ★ *mediocrity, co-dependence.*

The negative consequences of the parenting's first massive mistake or *parents and important others' way as almost the only way* may last a lifetime.

It may negatively impact certain children throughout their entire life, that is, throughout their own marriage and parenting style.

The parenting's first massive mistake or what Otto Rank calls *the Fear of Life* is part of what is at the deepest root causes of:

- ★ *marriage infidelities,*
- ★ *marriage instabilities,*
- ★ *domestic violence, bitter divorce...*

The Solution

The *Solution* to the *Fear of Life* negative consequences is to inspire *Gift-love lovers* to know why and how to *Balance their Fear of Life and their Fear of Death.*

In life, in love and in marriage:

- ★ *the common ground is the ideal playground,*
- ★ *the win-win is your marriage's ideal winning style,*
- ★ *the middle is your ideal pathway to wisdom.*

The *Solution* to the *Need-love lovers'* blind conformity and co-dependency is to know why and how to navigate smoothly back and forth between their need:

- ★ *for Belonging* and for relative *Independence,*
- ★ *for Balance* between their *External Authority and their own Inner Autonomy,*
- ★ *for Harmony between their loved one's Expectations and their personal Inclination.*

The *Balance* between *the Fear of Life and the Fear of Death* is the best way to go.

It is your best way of knowing why and how to *transcend* both the *Fear of Life and the Fear of Death.*

It is your best way of knowing why and how to enjoy and share the *middle* or what Otto Rank calls the *Artistic Creativity.*

When there is *Balance* between your *Fear of Life* and your *Fear of Death,* you will reach new and better ways of:

- ★ *seeing the world you live in,*
- ★ *being in the world you live in,*
- ★ *contributing to the world you live in.*

Dear spouses,
We each and all are, to some degree, the same important members
Of the same important family: the Human Family,
We each and all are divinely/spiritually/psychologically meant
To love one another as we love our own self,
We each and all are divinely/spiritually/psychologically meant
To step outside our own self to be a blessing to someone else.

It is natural and normal to love your loved ones
and important others,
It is natural and normal and necessary to love
All those who love you,
It should be natural and normal and necessary to love
Even those who hate you,
It should be natural and normal to forgive all,
Including your hurtful friends and worst enemies.

You are spiritually meant to meet and meltdown
To be *One,*
One with your own chosen *One*
Without losing your personal identity.
When you lose, for any reason, your self-identity
You have little or nothing left on the *Inside.*
Your *Inner Life* is so vital to your *Inner Peace,*
Your *Inner Peace* is so vital to your *Peace* with each other,
Your *Peace* with almost all, including your worst enemies.

You need to know why and how to love all,
Including all those who hate you,
You need to know why and how to forgive all,
Including all those who hurt you,
You need to know why and how
To refuse to be in love
With anyone else but your chosen love partner.
When you try to be in love and in intimacy with everyone,

You may end up having no one
To enjoy and share true *Love,*
Long-lasting *Peace* and *Intimacy* with each other.
This is easier said than done,
Especially for young people,
The choice is all yours,
Please, choose wisely.

Give More than Gift-Love

When *Gift-love* is all you give, you will be as dangerous to your own self as *Need-love lovers* are dangerous to their love partners.

The only difference is the name of the victim.

In *Need-love*, the victim is the innocent love partner.

In *Gift-love*, the victim is you, the *Gift-love giver.*

You can give the best you have, you can shake the earth and the 7 heavens for some people who may be still indifferent and distant...

For so many different reasons, so many different people may drift away as soon as possible. Once they know you, you are no longer the one and the only to them.

Imagine giving your heart and soul and spirit to someone who has none.

Their Own Story

In her book,
Tough Transitions: Navigating Your Way Through Difficult Times,
Elizabeth Harper Neeld talked about the following moving
ending of this marriage story.

We have been married for more than 30 years.

I had been his children's mother since they were preschoolers.

We have had four children on our own.

It has been my heart's delight to run a household and to love, raise and teach our eight children and be my husband's support in a high-profile public position.

But after more than thirty years of marriage, my husband left me for a younger woman and the world as I knew it was gone.

In the beginning, all I could do was cry.

My turning point was when I hosted my first party after the divorce was final.

I invited every person who has been supportive and kind to me: my dentist...my support group at church, my children…

I read Psalm 143 every night before I go to sleep.

Everything is not settled [yet]and...it is not easy.

But my faith is the bedrock I am standing on while I create my new life.

CHAPTER 9

Transcend Mature-Love

Step 9

Dear spouses, ***Step 9*** *to true Love and long lasting Peace*
and Intimacy every loving spouse needs to know is why and
how to transcend the natural and normal but too often too
limiting and too misleading ***Mature-Love.***

Dear spouses,
Mature Love lovers are the innocent victims of *the parenting's*
Third massive mistake
Or parents and their teens, adolescents...with no common way
Or what depth psychologist Carl G. Jung calls the *Empty Center.*

In his book, *The World of Love*, Isadore Schneider
Characterizes *Mature Love* lovers as two lovers
Trying to enjoy and share love *Fusion and Fulfillment*
Even when such love *Fusion* and *Fulfillment* is based upon
The day-to-day life business model, or:
**if you help me out with this, I will help you out with that,*
**if you do this for me, I will do that for you,*
**if you give this to me, I will give that to you.*

Mature Love lovers' biggest mistake is to believe
That money can buy anything;
In love and in marriage, there are things money cannot buy,
In love and in marriage, there are things
that defy all material things.
In love and in marriage, one of the most vital and memorable gifts

You can give to each other is to know
why and how to inspire them to:
★*awaken the positive side of their own Sleeping
Giant within that is in no other,*
★*treasure their own Priceless Inner Treasure that is in no other,*
★*share their own life's most favorite Love Song
that has never been sung before.*

True and long lasting *Love* for each other cannot be taught,
True and long lasting *Peace* and *Intimacy*
with each other cannot be bought,
True and long-lasting *Love* and *Peace* and
Intimacy can only be caught.
For true *Love* and long lasting *Peace* and *Intimacy* with each other
To be caught, they must spring up from the most sensitive strings
Of each other's innermost being;
True *Love* and long lasting *Peace* and *Intimacy* with each other
May defy all the gold and diamond mines of the whole world.

Their own Words

The Upanishads teaching said:

There is a light that shines brighter
than the sun...
the light in the highest 7 heavens.
It is the light
that shines within your heart.

Dear spouses,
The ninth *Vital* but too often missing *Life Saving Signal*
On the long road to true *Love* and long lasting *Peace and Intimacy*
Every loving spouse needs to know
Is
The powerful life-giving and life animating power
Of knowing why and how to enjoy and share
More than the natural and normal and necessary
But too often too limiting and misleading
MATURE LOVE.

You cannot enjoy and share true and long lasting:
**love for each other,*
**peace with each other,*
**intimacy with each other*
When all you give and all you receive and enjoy and share
Is the natural and normal and necessary
But too often too limiting and misleading
MATURE LOVE.

The ninth *Vital* but too often missing *Life Saving Signal*
On the long road to true *Love* and long lasting *Peace* and *Intimacy*
You need to know
Is

Your ever-increasing and never ending striving
To know why and how to enjoy and share more than:
**Need-Love,*
**Gift-Love,*
**Mature Love.*

Dear spouses,
The best would be loving spouses among you
May not know why and how
To enjoy and share true and long lasting:
**love for each other,*
**peace with each other,*
**intimacy with each other*
When one or both of you are facing the faceless face
Of the natural and normal and necessary
But often limiting and misleading
MATURE LOVE.

In his book, *The World of Love*, Isadore Schneider
Characterizes *Mature Love* as the *Fusion* and *Fulfillment*
Of two lovers even when such *Fusion* and *Fulfillment*
Are merely based on the two lovers' mere material needs
Or simply:
**if you help me out with this, I will help you out with that,*
**if you do this for me, I will do that for you,*
**if you give this to me, I will give that to you.*

To enjoy and share and celebrate
True *Love* and long lasting *Peace* and *Intimacy* with each other
Is to believe and behave and act and interact and react
As if whatever is yours is also mine,
As if whatever is mine is also yours,
As if as poet Pablo Neruda said,
Your hand in my chest is my own hand too.

Their own Words

Huston Smith said:

As human beings, we are only made
to surpass ourselves
and are truly ourselves
only when transcending ourselves.

Summary of the Chapter

Dear Spouses
It is very difficult or even impossible
To have the will and skills and wisdom
You need
To love with true and long lasting *Love,*
To be loved with true and long lasting *Love,*
To enjoy and share true and long lasting *Peace*
With each other,
To enjoy and share true and long lasting *Intimacy*
With each other
When one or both of you face the faceless face
Of the natural and normal but too often
Too limited, too limiting, too misleading...
Mature Love.
In life, in love, in marriage
There are things
The world's richest gold and diamond mines
Combined cannot buy.
True and long-lasting *Love* for each other,
True and long-lasting *Peace* with each other,
True and long-lasting *Intimacy* with each other
Can not be bought,
Can not be taught,

Cannot be imposed by force.
True love, inner peace so vital to peace with each other,
True and long lasting intimacy with each other
Can only be caught
By and through all you do and all you refuse to do
From the deepest recess of your innermost being.

Dear spouses, are you willing to fight with all your might to know why and how to:

- ★ *enjoy more than Mature love?*
- ★ *share more than Mature love?*
- ★ *celebrate more than Mature love?*

If *Yes* is your answer, you then need also to know why and how to:

- ★ *love each other with true and long lasting love,*
- ★ *enjoy and share true and long lasting peace,*
- ★ *enjoy and share true and long-lasting intimacy.*

Dear spouses,
If you are to enjoy and share true and long lasting:
★*love for each other,*
★*peace with each other,*
★*intimacy with each other*
You need to know why and how to inspire each other to:
★*awaken the positive side of their own Sleeping*
Giant within that is in no other,
★*treasure their own Priceless Inner Treasure that is in no other,*
★*share their most favorite Love Song that has never been sung before.*

Dear spouses, you each are, to some degree, unique.

You each are wonderfully made.

You each are made to make a positive difference:

- ★ *in your own life,*
- ★ *in each other's life,*
- ★ *in the lives of your loved ones and important others.*

If you do not know why and how to bring out the best there is deep within and all around both of you, no other extraordinary success in your life will help you compensate for your lack of:

- ★ *Inner Peace so vital to your Peace with each other,*

- ★ *true and long lasting Love for each other,*
- ★ *true and long-lasting Intimacy with each other.*

Dear spouse, there has never been someone exactly like you.

There will never be someone exactly like you.

You are unique.

You are wonderfully made.

You are made to make positive contributions:

- ★ *in your own life,*
- ★ *in each other's life,*
- ★ *in the life of your loved ones and important others.*

Your positive contributions to the quality of your marriage involve but encompass, by far, all material things.

For instance, are you willing and able to:

- ★ *accept and respect and tolerate your natural differences?*
- ★ *forgive each other and forget and heal and be whole?*
- ★ *tolerate each other's weaknesses such as one's naivety and vulnerability?*

Fight with all your might to know why and how to:

- ★ *identify your own Inner Calling,*
- ★ *inspire each other to answer their own Inner Calling,*
- ★ *inspire each other to enjoy and share their own Inner Calling.*

It is a divine /spiritual gift to know why and how to:

- ★ *love truly and live fully alive...*
- ★ *forgive, forget, heal, be whole, enjoy, share, celebrate...Ultimate Meaning...*
- ★ *welcome your own and each other's true, transcendent, infinite Self...*

But before you enjoy and share your *Inner Calling*, you need to know why and how to:

- *identify your own true identity,*
- *be true to your own true identity,*
- *become who truly you are meant to be.*

In life and in love and in marriage, you need to know why and how to be true to your own true *Self* if you are to know why and how to be *One* with one another without losing your personal identity.

Dear spouses, there is a place, an ineffable place, deep within and all around both of you, where each and every one of you is divine/spiritually/psychologically meant to be:

- *all-loving,*
- *all-knowing,*
- *all-powerful.*

That is the ineffable place where you are meant to meet and meltdown and be *One* with one another without losing your personal identity.

That place is the very place of true *Love and long lasting Peace and Intimacy* where you are meant to:

- *love all those who love you,*
- *love even all those who hate you,*
- *forgive all those who hurt you.*

The Problem

Dear spouses, the ninth major barrier to true *Love* and long lasting *Peace* and *Intimacy* every loving spouse needs to know is why and how to:

- *prevent the natural and normal but often liming and misleading Mature Love,*
- *or confront the natural and normal but often limiting and misleading Mature Love,*

- *and overcome the natural and normal but often limiting and misleading Mature Love.*

Mature Love lovers' business-like love style is due to:

- *the parenting third massive mistake,*
- *or parents and their grown-up children with no common way or no way at all,*
- *or what depth psychologist Carl G. Jung calls the Empty Center.*

It is easier to face the faceless face of *the Fear of Life and the Fear of Death* than *the bottomless abyss of nothingness created by the Empty Center.*

The *Empty Center* is probably at the root causes of what Viktor E. Frankl calls:

- *the existential vacuum,*
- *the existential frustration,*
- *the frustrated will to meaning, to power, to money, to pleasure at its lowest level,*

The *Empty Center* is a major barrier to:

- *the healthy and free and fully alive innocent Inner Child in both of you,*
- *the powerful life-giving and life animating power of your Fulfillment,*
- *the Inner Peace so vital your Peace with each other.*

With the *Empty Center,* you have:

- *no theology,*
- *no ideology,*
- *no solid worldview,*
- *no philosophy of life,*
- *no shared values,*
- *no time-tested ways of life...*

In the Empty Center, all you have is:

- *I, me, mine, myself...*

- ★ *my way or no other way...*
- ★ *self aggrandizement, megalomania...*

Dear spouses,
You cannot enjoy and share true and long lasting:
★*love for each other,*
★*peace with each other,*
★*intimacy with each other*
When one or both of you do not know why and how
To welcome and enjoy and share each other:
★*true Self,*
★*transcendent Self,*
★*infinite Self.*

The Solution

The *Solution to Mature Love lovers'* limiting and misleading deep-rooted belief that money can buy anything is to inspire them to be aware and convinced that:

- ★ *there are things in life money cannot buy...*
- ★ *money cannot buy love, respect, trust...*
- ★ *money cannot buy Peace and Intimacy with each other...*

For instance, all the money of the whole world cannot buy you true and long lasting:

- ★ *healthy self-love,*
- ★ *love for each other,*
- ★ *peace and intimacy with each other.*

Dear Spouses,
Learn why and how to give more than *Mature Love,*
Learn why and how to require more than *Mature Love.*
To love truly is to be in touch with the best there is
Deep within both of you,

To love truly is to be deeply touched by the best there is
All around both of you.
To love truly is to know why and how
To enjoy and share and celebrate
The ineffable something more and bigger and better
Between the best there is
Deep within and all around both of you.

To love truly is to know why and how
To forgive, forget, heal and be whole,
To love truly is to know why and how
To love all those who love you,
To love truly is to know why and how
To love all those who hate you,
To love truly is to know why and how
To forgive all those who hurt you.

To love truly is to know why and how
To love your own self first with true and long lasting
Healthy self-love,
To love truly is to know why and how
To love each other with true and long lasting
Healthy self-love,
To love truly is to know why and how
To love each other with spiritual love,
To love truly is to know why and how
To love each other with unconditional love,
To love truly is to know why and how
To hear what is not said,
To love truly is to know why and how
To read between the lines,
To love truly is to know why and how
To see in each other more than an eye can see.

True love is your smoothest and straightest road
To the best there is still in all there has been,
To the best there is in all there is here and now,
To the best there will be in all there is about to be.

Mature Love can be a blinding type of love.

Mature Love can be a selfish type of love.

Mature Love can be a self-destructive type of love.

Like the deadly cancerous cells, *Mature Love* can be:

- ⋆ *a deadly hidden disease,*
- ⋆ *a fatal hidden killer.*

Get rid of it.
Stay away from it.

The following story is a literary example of *Mature Love that* turns out to be fatal for both lovers.

Their Own Story

In his romantic novel, *The Red and The Black (1830),*
French novelist Stendhal (Henry Beyle) main character,
the young Julien Sorel is engaged in a passionate relationship
with the mayor's wife, Madame de Renal.

Once caught, he was condemned to death.

While awaiting his execution, Julien Sorel's passionate love
for Madame de Renal rose to another level.

And Julien Sorel died while being loved by Madame de Renal too.

Three days after Julien Sorel's execution,
Madame de Renal gives her children her last kiss
and follows Julien Sorel, her heart has given away too.

Sorel's story is proof that *Mature Love* can also be a self-destructive type of love too. It can be deadly for both lovers. It can be harmful to their children and their other loved ones and important others.

In his book, *Love in the Western World,*
Denis de Rougemont said:

Nine out of ten times,
the great loves in Western Literature
take the form of adultery.

He went on as far as to state that:

It is obvious that...man is drawn
to what destroys the happiness of married couples
at least as much as to anything that ensures it.

Dear spouse,
When the visible, the tangible, the ponderable...
Is your highest aim,
When you live as if the whole world
Were merely material,
That may be one of your smoothest and roads to your:
**wounded innocent Inner Child,*
**deep and unfathomable Inner Void,*
**ineffable and unbearable Pain of Inner Emptiness.*

No one and nothing material can help you:
★*accept and respect and protect your innocent Inner Child,*
★*fulfill your deep and unfathomable Inner Void,*
★*end your ineffable and unbearable Pain of Inner Emptiness.*
Only *divine/spiritual love, healthy self-love, unconditional love,*
Forgiveness, healing, wholeness, ultimate meaning...
Can help you:
★*love truly with your true, transcendent, infinite Self,*
★*love truly each other with your true, transcendent, infinite Self,*
★*love almost all with true love, including your worst enemies.*

The novelist Henry Beyle, known as Stendhal, said:

It is a wasting of time
to spend one's own time
talking about how the great
became great.

Dear spouses, as Stendhal suggests, be aware and convinced that there is greatness within each and every one of you and within each and everyone you meet including the hopeless, the helpless, the homeless, the needy, the hungry...

Therefore, fight, day and night, with all your might for your:

- ★ *own personal greatness,*
- ★ *each other's greatness,*
- ★ *true Love and long-lasting Peace and Intimacy in your marriage.*

PART IV

How to Share the 3 Types of true Love and Long Lasting Peace and Intimacy every Would be an Excellent Spouse Needs to Know?

...whatever name our logic may give to the truth of human unity, the fact can never be ignored that we realize ourselves in others, and this is the definition of love. This love gives us the testimony of the great whole, which is the complete and final truth of man. The Spirit of love, dwelling in the boundless realm of the surplus, emancipates our consciousness from the illusory separateness of self...

(Rabindranath Tagore, Indian writer)

Dear spouses,

The 3 rock-solid founding and building blocks
Of true and long lasting:
★love for each other,
★peace with each other,
★intimacy with each other
are:
Healthy self-love, Spiritual love, Unconditional love.

Healthy self-love, Spiritual love,
Unconditional love
Are what you need first and the most
If you are to know why and how
To enjoy and share and celebrate
True and long lasting:
★love for each other,
★peace with each other,
★intimacy with each other.

Healthy self-love, Spiritual love,
unconditional love
Are what you need first and the most
If you are to know why and how to:
★love your own self with healthy self-love,
★love each other with true love,
★love each other with true and long lasting peace and intimacy,
★love all those who love you,
★love all those who hate you,
★forgive all those who hurt you.

True and unconditional love for your own *Self,*
True and unconditional love for each other's true *Self,*
True and unconditional love for all including
Your worst enemies' true *Self* is what you need first

If you are to see *all the men and all the women*
Of the whole world as the same important members
Of the same important family: the Human Family.
As human beings,
We each and all are feeble and fallible and vulnerable,
Therefore, what is said here is easier said than done
For you and for me and for each and everyone of all as a whole.

CHAPTER 10

Share Healthy Self-Love

Step 10

Dear spouses, ***Step 10*** *to true Love and long lasting Peace*
and Intimacy every loving spouse needs to know is why and
how to love your own self with true and long lasting
Healthy Self-Love.

Dear spouses,
The only person you can truly control is you
And only when you know why and how to:
**be deeply in touch with your own true Self,*
**be deeply touched by your own true Self,*
**love your own self with true and long-lasting healthy self-love.*

Ancient Chinese philosopher and teacher, Confucius, said:
Your children are not your children,
Your children are the children of their time.
Kahlil Gibran, echoed Confucius when he said:
Parents are the bow, children the arrow.
Both Confucius and Gibran
Mean that parents need, at the right time, to let their children go,
Parents need to let their children be
The very captains of their own destiny.

Healthy self-love is one of your smoothest roads
To true and long lasting:
**love and aliveness,*
**forgiveness, healing, wholeness, ultimate meaning...*
**inner peace, inner autonomy, self-navigation.*

Healthy self-love is what you need first
If you are to know why and how
To *transcend* your natural and normal
But too often too limiting and too misleading:
Need-love, Gift-love, Mature love.
To enjoy and share *healthy self-love*,
You need to know why and how to:
★*transcend your limiting and misleading lower self,*
★*enjoy and share the emergence of your own true Self,*
★*enjoy and share each other's transcendent and infinite Self.*

Their own Words

Poet Dale Wimbrow said:

We can fool the whole world and get pats
on the back as we pass.
But our final reward will be heartaches
and tears if we've cheated the guy in the glass.

Dear spouses,
The tenth *Vital* but too often missing *Life Saving Signal*
On the long road to true *Love* and long lasting *Peace* and *Intimacy*
Every loving spouse need to know
Is
The powerful life-giving and animating power of
HEALTHY SELf-LOVE.

You cannot enjoy and share true and long lasting:
**love for each other,*
**peace with each other,*
**intimacy with each other*
When one or both of you do not know why and how
To love your own *Self* with
HEALTHY SELF-LOVE.

The tenth *Vital* but too often missing *Life Saving Signal*
On the long road to true *Love* and long lasting *Peace* and *Intimacy*
You need to know
Is
Your ever-increasing and never ending striving
For wisdom, you need to know why and how
To enjoy and share the emergence of your own:
**true Self,*
**transcendent Self,*
**infinite Self.*

Dear spouses,
The best would be loving spouses among you
May not know why and how
To enjoy and share true and long lasting:
★*love for each other,*
★*peace with each other,*
★*intimacy with each other*
As long as one or both of you
Do not know why and how
To love your own self with
HEALTHY SELF-LOVE.

If you are to enjoy and share
True and long lasting:
★*love for each other,*
★*peace with each other,*
★*intimacy with each other*
You need first to know why and how
To love your own self with true and long lasting
HEALTHY SELF-LOVE.

Their own Words

William Shakespeare said:

If you love and get hurt,
love more.
If you love more and hurt more,
love even more.
If you love even more
and get hurt even more,
love some more
until it hurts no more.

Summary of the Chapter

Dear Spouses,
It is very difficult or even impossible
To have the will and skills and wisdom
You need
To love with true and long lasting *Love,*
To be loved with true and long lasting *Love,*
To enjoy and share true and long lasting *Peace*
With each other,
To enjoy and share true and long lasting *Intimacy*
With each other
When one or both of you face the faceless face
Of the too limited and too limiting,
And too misleading relations and interactions
Without ***Healthy Self-love.***
If you do not love your own self with *Healthy Self-love,*
No one will love you with true and long lasting *Love,*
No one will love you with true and long lasting *Peace,*
No one will love you with true and long-lasting *Intimacy.*
Healthy self-love precedes and prepares

Your ability to:
★*read each other between the lines,*
★*see in each other more than eye can see,*
★*hear each other beyond the spoken words.*

Dear spouses, are you willing to fight with all your might to know why and how to:

- *love your own self with true and long-lasting healthy self-love?*
- *love each other with true and long-lasting healthy self-love?*
- *enjoy and share true and long-lasting healthy self-love?*

If *Yes* is your answer, you then need also to know why and how to welcome the emergence of:

- *your own true Self,*
- *each other's true Self,*
- *each other's true, transcendent, infinite Self.*

As spiritual beings, you are divinely/spiritually meant to be:

- *all-loving,*
- *all-knowing,*
- *all-powerful.*

You need to know why and how to be *all-loving, all-knowing, and all-powerful* if you are to be open and receptive to the will and the wisdom you need to:

- *love all those who love you,*
- *love even all those who hate you,*
- *forgive all those who hurt you.*

To succeed, you need to be aware and convinced that there is always:

- *something more,*
- *something bigger,*
- *something better.*

Dear spouses, know why and how to free each other from the limiting and misleading:

- *meaninglessness,*
- *mindlessness,*
- *shortsightedness.*

Dear spouses,
The emergence of your own true Self frees you
from the dark and ugly and stubborn and repressed
and rejected and almost forgotten but often present
side of your Personal Unconscious.

You need to know why and how to get rid of the parts of your *Personality* you are not very proud of.

You need to know why and how to get rid of the parts of your personality you do not want to remember, acknowledge, share...

To enjoy and share a happy marriage, you need to know why and how to get rid of the dark and ugly and stubborn side of your own and each other's *Personal Unconscious.*

To succeed, you must listen, understand, internalize, co-own what your world's great religious and spiritual traditions and collective wisdom have been telling you all along.

Once you succeed, you will be well equipped and ready to see:

- ★ *a message beneath every mess,*
- ★ *your adversity as a great university,*
- ★ *a star beyond every scar.*

Dear spouses, there is a place, an ineffable place, deep within both of you where you are spiritually meant to meet and meltdown and be *One* with full *Self-awareness:*

- ★ *one with your own true Self,*
- ★ *one with each other's true Self,*
- ★ *one with everyone's else true Self, including your worst enemies.*

Healthy self-love is one of your first smoothest and straightest roads to:

- ★ *true love, aliveness, inner peace, and long lasting intimacy with each other,*

- ★ *forgiveness, healing, wholeness, a meaningful, peaceful, and purposeful life,*
- ★ *the emergence of your own true, transcendent, infinite Self.*

When you welcome the emergence of your own true *Self,* you will realize why and how you have to:

- ★ *avoid being your own worst enemy,*
- ★ *be and remain your own best friend,*
- ★ *love your own Self first if you are to love anyone else.*

Your ability to love your own self with *Healthy Self-love* precedes and prepares your ability to:

- ★ *love truly, live fully alive...*
- ★ *forgive, forget, heal, be whole...*
- ★ *enjoy and share a meaningful, peaceful, purposeful, fulfilled life...*

Your healthy self-love is vital to your *Inner Peace.*

Inner Peace is *the Panacea* or universal remedy against all man-made tragedies, including domestic violence.

Love Your Own Self With Healthy Self-Love

In interpreting the Bhagavad Gita,
Sri Aurobindo said:

Real self-knowledge can only come
when man perceives
that the Self in him and the Self in others
are being, and this Self is something higher
than
the ego---an infinite, an impersonal, a universal
existence in whom all move and have their being.

Their own Story

The Power of Healthy Self-love

Solomon was one of the most powerful biblical Kings.

He was also one of the richest men who ever lived.

He had many wives and many concubines.

But Solomon knelt down before one woman.

He knelt down with a smile on his face all his way down.

That woman was the Queen of Sheba.

What did the powerful and wealthy King
Solomon see in the Queen of Sheba?

What was so special about the Queen of Sheba that was lacking
in Solomon's many other wives and concubines?

The answer seems simple.

The Queen of Sheba had Healthy Self-love. She had an authentic *Self.*

The Queen of Sheba did not love Solomon merely
because he was a powerful King.

The Queen of Sheba did not love Solomon solely
because he was the richest man who ever lived.

The Queen of Sheba loved Solomon as an equal.

That was it.

That was enough.

That made all the difference.

As part of his own life, Solomon himself was a wise man.
He gave more attention, thoughts, and consideration to wisdom and understanding than a kingdom and material possessions.

"How much better is to get wisdom than gold..." (Proverb, 16-16)

The Problem

Dear spouses, the tenth major barrier to true *Love* and long lasting *Peace* and *Intimacy* every loving spouse needs to know is why and how to:

- ★ *acknowledge the dark and ugly side of your personal Unconscious,*
- ★ *integrate the dark and ugly side of your Personal Unconscious,*
- ★ *get rid of the dark and ugly side of your Personal Unconscious.*

The dark and ugly and stubborn side of your Personal Unconscious is a major barrier to your *Healthy Self-Love.*

Depth psychologists tell us that our *Ego Unconscious* casts out a *Shadow.*

Our *Shadow* is the parts of our *Personality* that have been repressed and rejected because of their cognitive and emotional dissonance with our *Conscious* attitudes.

The dark and ugly traits of our *Personal Unconscious* have a life on their own.

They are outside the control of our *Conscious attitudes.*

As "*Partial Autonomous Systems*," they may pop up on their own to invade our *Conscious attitudes.*

The *Shadow* symbolizes our personal traits and features that are contrary to our social norms.

Our *Shadow* is the unconscious side of our *Ego's* operations.

According to Jung, our *Shadow* is *the heart of the darkness within the Ego.*

Our *Shadow is the very definition of human evil* as it is played in myths and stories.

What your *Ego Consciousness* rejects becomes your *Shadow.*

Your *Shadow* is your personal traits and features that are incompatible with your *Conscious Ego and your social norms and customs.*

Their own Words

In his famous novel entitled, *Anna Karinena,*
Russian writer,
Leo Tolstoi describes the tensions and contradictions
between the *Conscious Ego* and the *Shadow.*

Anna was caught up in passionate adulterous love.

She was caught up between her legal marriage and her profane
but passionate love for her boyfriend.

Anna was a victim of forces beyond her own control.

She was tormented by love, her traditional marriage,
she can neither abandon nor enjoy.

Cast out by her society, separated from her son, Anna Karenina's life was heading to an unbearable tragedy.

Her marriage was pitiable. She was handed over in a marriage to a man twenty years older than her.

Despite all the social and spiritual consequences, Anna's attachment to her boyfriend, Vronsky, bursts beyond the bounds of an acceptable secret between a young officer and a married woman.

Anna's love cannot be managed. She lived in a perpetual anguish between her passionate love and guilty feelings.

She was torn apart between a passionate love that gives meaning to her life and a traditional convention that cast her out from societal norms.

She doesn't want to give up her passionate love and she cannot feel happy with it.

The Solution

The *Solution* to the lack of *Healthy Self-love* is to know why and how to bring to life and to integrate and then to get rid of the dark and ugly and stubborn side of your own and then of each other's *Personal Unconscious.*

How to integrate the dark and ugly side of the *Personal Unconscious* into the *Conscious* attitudes is a personal struggle.

You have to fight for it with all your might, almost on your own.

To succeed, you must know why and how to *Harmonize* the natural and normal pairs of your own *Personal inner Opposites,* such as your:

- ★ *Consciousness and Unconscious,*
- ★ *Ego and Shadow,*

- ★ *Persona-mask and true and total Personality.*

When you know why and how to integrate the dark and ugly side of your own *Personal Unconscious* into your *Conscious* attitudes, you will be a new and a better person. You will rise above the average person. You will find new and better ways of:

- ★ *seeing the world you live in,*
- ★ *seeing your own place in the world,*
- ★ *dealing with each other with true love, trust, and compassion.*

Once you come out of the dark and ugly side of your own *Personal Unconscious,* you will be fully aware of what pushes certain people to:

- ★ *selfishness,*
- ★ *self-centeredness,*
- ★ *haterade, including self-hatred.*

But to come out of the dark, ugly, and stubborn side of your *Personal Unconscious* is only possible after your own:

- ★ *in-depth soul searching,*
- ★ *moral courage, effort, and struggle,*
- ★ *healthy self-criticism.*

Dear spouses, the narrower the gap between your natural and normal *Persona-mask* and your true and total *Personality,* the greater your opportunity to enjoy and share:

- ★ *healthy self-criticism,*
- ★ *healthy self-acceptance,*
- ★ *healthy self-love.*

Healthy Self-love is your first and one of your best ways to your own:

- ★ *true Self,*
- ★ *transcendent Self,*
- ★ *infinite Self.*

The *Emergence* of your true, transcendent, infinite *Self* is vital to your ability to:

- ★ *love truly and live fully alive...*
- ★ *forgive, forget, heal, be whole...*
- ★ *enjoy and share a meaningful, peaceful, purposeful life...*

Your ever-increasing and never ending striving for wholeness is your pathway to the wisdom you need to know why and how to enjoy and share *Oneness* with full *Self-awareness:*

- ★ *oneness with your loved ones and important others,*
- ★ *oneness between your knowledge/skills and innate talent,*
- ★ *oneness between what you have to do and what you are called to do,*
- ★ *oneness with your own and each other's true, transcendent, infinite Self,*

Dear spouses,
Healthy self-love is the first rock solid founding block,
Healthy self-love is the first rock-solid building block
Of your *Inner Peace* so vital to your *Peace* with:
★*each other,*
★*your loved ones,*
★*your important others.*

Your healthy self-love is vital
To your true Love and long lasting Peace with your own:
★*true Self,*
★*spouse's true Self,*
★*loved ones and important others' true Self.*

Your healthy self-love is your first
Rock-solid founding and building block
Of true *Love* and long lasting *Peace and Intimacy*
With each other.

Your healthy self-love is vital
To your marriage stability,

To the outcome of your ever-increasing striving for
ONENESS:
★*oneness with your own true Self,*
★*oneness with each other's true Self,*
★*oneness with everyone else's true Self.*

Their own Words

Harvard professor of psychology,
William James said:

...there is but one cause of human failure.
And that is man's lack of faith in his
true Self.

Your healthy self-love is your pathway to your ability to:

- ★ *identify your own true identity,*
- ★ *be true to your own true identity,*
- ★ *become who truly you are meant to be.*

Their Own Story

In his book, *The Richest Man Who Ever Lived: King Solomon's Secrets To Success, Wealth And Happiness,* Steve K. Scott, shares one of his own life-changing experiences in the following words.

When Steve was only 23 years old, one of his bosses told him:

Steve, you are the single greatest disappointment in my life...

You will never succeed in marketing...

You have 20 minutes to clean out your desk...

Steve rather saw his own life's adversity as his greatest university.

Before, he was earning less than half the income
of the average American wage earner.

His income rose from $18,000 per year to more than $7.000.000 per year.

Steve finally became:
★*a multimillionaire businessman,*
★*a best selling author,*
★*a popular international motivational speaker,*
★*a specialist of personal growth, professional*
development, and high performance.

CHAPTER 11

Share Spiritual Love

Step 11

Dear spouses, ***Step 11*** *to true Love and long lasting Peace and Intimacy every loving spouse needs to know is why and how to love your own self, love each other and love all, including your hurtful friends and foes with true and long lasting* ***Spiritual Love.***

Dear spouses,
If one or both of you do not know why and how
To love each other with *Spiritual Love,*
You won't be able to know why and how
To be in touch with and be deeply touched by
Each other's true, transcendent, infinite *Self.*
Nineteenth-century French romantic poet,
Alfred de Lamartine, said:
I have opponents but I have no enemies,
I am a co-citizen of every thinking soul,
Truth, that's my country.

Most of our day-to-day life fears and failures
And frictions and frustrations,
Most of our day-to-day life uncertainties
And perplexities and anxieties,
Most of our day-to-day life emotional instabilities
Are due to our *Non-alignment* with *the Spirit or the Divine Order.*
If you are to be in *Alignment* with *the Spirit or the Divine Order,*
If you are to *Harmonize* the natural pairs
of your personal *inner Opposites,*

If you are to be in *Peace* with *your own true*
Self and with each other's true Self,
If you are to be in touch with and be deeply by
your own and each other's Higher Self
You need to know why and how to:
**transcend your reasoning mind,*
**follow your Divine/Spiritual Guidance,*
**enjoy and share your common Universal Heritage.*
The purer and more peaceful your spirit,
the purer and more powerful
The *Emanations you* send to your own self
and to each other and to the world,
The lower and the poorer your spirit, the lower and the poorer
The *Emanations you* send to your own self
and to each other and to the world.
The mystery of your natural and normal
life transcends your rational mind,
The mystery of the inner world and your outer world
Transcends what your reasoning mind can comprehend.

Their own Words

World bestselling author, Ralph Waldo Trine said:

This is the Spirit of Infinite Love.
The moment we recognize ourselves as one with it,
we become so filled with love that we see
only the good in all.
...when we realize that we all are one
with this Infinite Spirit, then we realize that
we all are one with each other.

Dear spouses,
The eleventh *Vital* but too often missing *Life Saving Signal*
On the long road to true *Love* and long lasting *Peace* and *Intimacy*
Every spouse needs to know
Is
The powerful life-giving and animating power
Of knowing why and how to:
⋆*love your own self with spiritual love,*
⋆*love each other with spiritual love,*
⋆*love all, including your worst enemies, with spiritual love.*

You cannot enjoy and share true and long lasting:
⋆*love for each other,*
⋆*peace with each other,*
⋆*intimacy with each other*
If one or both of you do not know why and how
To love your own self and love each other and love all with
SPIRITUAL LOVE.

The eleventh *Vital* but too often missing *Life Saving Signal*
On the long road to true *Love* and long lasting *Peace and Intimacy*
You need to know
Is
Your ever-increasing and never ending striving
To know why and how to:
⋆*love your own self with spiritual love,*
⋆*love each other with spiritual love,*
⋆*love all, including your worst enemies, with*
SPIRITUAL LOVE.

Dear spouses,
The best would be loving spouses among you
May not know why and how
To enjoy and share true and long lasting:
**love for each other,*
**peace with each other,*
**intimacy with each other*
When one or both of you do not know why and how to:
**love your own self with spiritual love,*
**love each other with spiritual love,*
**love all, including your worst enemies, with*
SPIRITUAL LOVE.

There is a place, an ineffable place,
Deep within each and every one of us
Where we each and all are divinely/spiritually
Meant to be whole,
Where we each and all are divinely/spiritually
Meant to meet and to meltdown and to be *One,*
One with the *One* within and all around every one of us,
One with our own true *Self,*
One with our own spouse's transcendent *Self,*
One with everyone else's transcendent *Self,*
One with even our own hurtful friends and foes' transcendent *Self.*

We each and all are divinely/spiritually meant to be:
**all-loving,*
**all-knowing,*
**all-powerful.*

Their Own Words

In interpreting the Bhagavad Gita,
Sri Aurobindo said:

When one discovers the spirit within him,
he realizes that he is one with…
all other fellows human beings.
Only then...can love become the law of life,
peace and harmony be established...on earth.
Love [is] a mutual recognition of human brotherhood,
[Love is] a living sense of human oneness...
[Love is] a practice of human oneness in thought, feeling, and life.

Summary of the Chapter

Dear Spouses,
It is very difficult or even impossible
To have the will and skills and wisdom
You need
To love with true and long-lasting *Love,*
To be loved with true and long-lasting *Love,*
To enjoy and share true and long-lasting *Peace*
With each other,
To enjoy and share true and long lasting *Intimacy*
With each other
When one or both of you
Are in disconnection with the Spirit.
You are meant to transcend your own lower self,
You are meant to transcend each other's lower self,
You are meant to be *One* with the best there is
Deep within and all around each other.
Your *Oneness* with full *Self-awareness*
With your own transcendent *Self,*

With each other's transcendent *Self*,
With everyone else's transcendent *Self*
Including your hurtful friends and worst enemies
Is your smooth and straight road
To *Spiritual Awakening*, to *Spiritual Love,*
To your ability to see all men and all women
Of the whole world as the same important members
Of the same important family: the Human Family.

Dear spouses, are you willing to fight with all your might to know why and how to:

- ★ *love your own self with true and long-lasting Spiritual love?*
- ★ *love each other with true and long-lasting Spiritual love?*
- ★ *enjoy and share Spiritual love with all, including your hurtful friends and foes?*

If *Yes* is your answer, you then need also to know why and how to start your ever increasing and never ending striving for *Oneness* with full *Self-awareness:*

- ★ *oneness with your own transcendent Self,*
- ★ *oneness with each other's transcendent Self,*
- ★ *oneness with everyone else's transcendent Self.*

Dear spouses,
If you are to enjoy and share true and long lasting:
★*love for each other,*
★*peace with each other,*
★*intimacy with each other*
You need to know why and how to:
★*love your own self with true and long lasting Spiritual love,*
★*love each other with true and long lasting Spiritual love,*
★*love all, including your worst enemies, with*
true and long-lasting Spiritual love.

Love your own self with true and long-lasting spiritual love.

Love each other with true and long-lasting Spiritual love.

Love all with true and long-lasting Spiritual love.

Inspire each other to be aware and convinced of the ineffable presence of the *Larger* than *Life:*

- ★ *deep within every one of you,*
- ★ *all around every one of you,*

- ★ *in between the best there is within and all around both of you.*

Inspire each other to know why and how to be in touch with and be deeply touched by the powerful life-giving and life animating power of the everlasting impulse of the *Spirit.*

Inspire each other to know why and how to meet and meltdown and be *One* with one another without losing your personal identity.

Spiritual love for each other provides you with new and better ways of seeing and understanding:

- ★ *the world you live in,*
- ★ *your own place in the world,*
- ★ *each other's infinite possibilities.*

The *Harmony* between the natural and normal pairs of your personal inner *Opposites* is one of the rock-solid founding blocks of your true and long lasting:

- ★ *healthy self-love,*
- ★ *true and long lasting love for each other,*
- ★ *true and long-lasting peace and intimacy with each other.*

In life and in love and in marriage, when there is no *Harmony* between the natural and normal pairs of your personal *inner Opposite*, there will be no:

- ★ *true and long lasting Inner Peace so vital to Peace with one another,*
- ★ *true and long lasting Healthy Self-love for each other,*
- ★ *true and long-lasting Intimacy with each other.*

The Problem

Dear spouses, the eleventh major barrier to true *Love* and long-lasting *Peace and Intimacy* every loving spouse needs to know is why and how to inspire each other to:

- ★ *protect the vital but too vulnerable innocent Inner Child within both of you,*
- ★ *fulfill the deep and unfathomable Inner Void within one or both of you,*
- ★ *end the unbearable Pain of Inner Emptiness within one or both of you.*

The *lack of Spiritual Love* for each other is due to:

- ★ *the deeply wounded innocent Inner Child within one or both of you,*
- ★ *the deep and unfathomable possible Inner Void within one or both of you,*
- ★ *the unbearable possible Pain of Inner Emptiness within one or both of you.*

The *wounded* innocent *Inner Child* within one or both of you is the first major barrier to your ability to know why and how to:

- ★ *love your own self with spiritual love,*
- ★ *love each other with spiritual love,*
- ★ *love all, including your worst enemies, with spiritual love.*

The wounded innocent *Inner Child* within one or both of you is at the root cause of what psychologist of *Artistic Creativity,* Otto Rank, and depth psychologist, Carl G. Jung, call:

- ★ *the Fear of Life,*
- ★ *the Fear of Death,*
- ★ *the Empty Center.*

The *Fear of Life, the Fear of Death, and the Empty Center* are incompatible with the will and skills and wisdom you need to *transcend* the too often too limiting and misleading:

- ★ *need-love,*
- ★ *gift-love,*
- ★ *mature love.*

For instance, when you create *the Empty Center*, your *Ego's* main concern will only be:

- ★ *does it work?*
- ★ *what is in it for me?*
- ★ *how can I get the best and the most out of every situation?*

In life, in love, and in marriage, the *middle* is your ideal pathway to wisdom.

Your wisdom is vital to the full expression of your heartfelt true and long lasting:

- ★ *love for each other,*
- ★ *peace with each other,*
- ★ *intimacy with each other.*

The deep and unfathomable possible *Inner Void* within one or both of you is your second major barrier to the full expression of your heartfelt true and long lasting:

- ★ *spiritual love for your own self,*
- ★ *spiritual love for each other,*
- ★ *spiritual love for all, including your own worst enemies.*

The deep and unfathomable possible *Inner Void* within one or both of you may lead you to what psychiatrist and logo-therapist, Viktor E. Frankl, calls:

- ★ *the existential vacuum,*
- ★ *the existential frustration,*
- ★ *the frustrated will to meaning, to power, to money, to pleasure at its lowest level.*

The ineffable and unbearable possible *Pain of Inner Emptiness* within one or both of you is your third major barrier to the full expression of your heartfelt true and long-lasting:

- ★ *spiritual love for your own self,*
- ★ *spiritual love for each other,*

- *spiritual love for all, including your own worst enemies.*

Due to the parenting 3 massive mistakes, certain children may experience what the psychologist, Otto Rank, and depth psychologist, Carl G. Jung, call:

- *the Fear of Life,*
- *the Fear of Death,*
- *the Empty Center.*

These 3 negative consequences of the parenting 3 massive mistakes are 3 major barriers to true and long lasting:

- *love for each other,*
- *peace with each other,*
- *intimacy with each other.*

Dear spouses, sometimes, the fate of your marriage is already decided long before you grow up and fall in love and get married.

Indeed, the quality of your education in general and your parenting outcomes, in particular, determine your ability to enjoy and share and celebrate true *Love* and long-lasting *Peace* and *Intimacy* with each other.

How you prevent or confront and overcome one of the parenting 3 massive mistakes will determine your genuine openness and receptivity to true *Love* and long-lasting *Peace* and *Intimacy* in your marriage.

The Solution

The *Solution* to the lack of *Spiritual Love* of one or both of you is to inspire each other to know why and how to:

- *protect the healthy and free and fully alive innocent Inner Child in both of you,*

- ★ *fulfill the deep and unfathomable possible Inner Void within one or both of you,*
- ★ *end the unbearable possible Pain of Inner Emptiness* within one or both of you.

These 3 vital steps to your marriage's stability and happiness are discussed in detail in Part I, chapter 1, chapter 2, and chapter 3 of this book.

CHAPTER 12

Share Unconditional Love

Step 12

Dear spouses, ***Step 12*** *to true Love and long lasting Peace and Intimacy every loving spouse needs to know is why and how to love your own self and love each other with true and long lasting* ***Unconditional Love.***

Dear spouses,
When you know why and how to:
**love your own self with true and Unconditional Love,*
**love each other with true and Unconditional Love,*
**love all, including your enemies, with true and Unconditional Love,*
You may bring the whole world near to
your heart and soul and spirit,
You may make the whole world dear to
your heart and soul and spirit,
You may make the whole world home to
your heart and soul and spirit.

Some of the world great religious and spiritual traditions,
Some of the world great collective wisdom,
Some of the world great depth psychologists and psychoanalysts
Tell us that there is a place, an ineffable place,
Deep within and all around
Each and every one of us all as a whole
Where we each and all
Are divinely/spiritually/psychologically
Meant to meet and to meltdown and to be *One,*
One with one another
Without losing our personal identity.

When we are true to the ineffable:
**something more,*
**something bigger,*
**something better*
All around each and every one
Of us a all as a whole,
We will be true to the ineffable:
**something more,*
**something bigger,*
**something better*
Deep within each and every one
Of us all as a whole.

Dear spouses,
When we go into the deepest layers
Of our collective *Unconscious,*
We will realize that psychologically,
We each and all are One with one another,
We each and all are divinely/spiritually
Meant to know why and how
To enjoy and share the divine
Within each and every one of us all.

When we see one another
As righteous and truthful and good,
We will see righteousness
Truthfulness and goodness
Within each and every one of us all.
When our heart and soul and spirit
Are open and receptive
To true love with our own true *Self*
To true love with everyone else's true *Self,*
We will send true *Love* and *Peace*
To each and every one of us all as a whole.

Their own Words

Russian writer, Leo Tolstoi, said:

When you love someone, you love the person
as they are and not as you'd like them to be.

Dear spouses,
The twelfth *Vital* but too often missing *Life Saving Signal*
On the long road to true *Love and long lasting Peace and Intimacy*
Every loving spouse needs to know
Is
The powerful life-giving and life animating power
Of knowing why and how to love one another
With true and long lasting:
UNCONDITIONAL LOVE.

You cannot enjoy and share true and long lasting:
⋆*love for one another,*
⋆*peace with one another,*
⋆*intimacy with one another*
When one or both of you do not know why and how
To love each other with true and long lasting:
UNCONDITIONAL LOVE.

The twelfth *Vital* but too often missing *Life Saving Signal*
On the long road to true *Love* and long lasting *Peace* and *Intimacy*
You need to know
Is
Your ever-increasing and never ending striving
For the will and skills and wisdom, you need
To know why and how to:
⋆*love your own self with unconditional love,*
⋆*love each other with unconditional love,*
⋆*love all, including your opponents with unconditional love.*

Dear spouses,
The best would be loving spouses among you
May not know why and how to:
★*love their own self with unconditional love,*
★*love each other with unconditional love,*
★*love all, including their hurtful friends and foes, with*
UNCONDITIONAL LOVE.

To love with true and long lasting
UNCONDITIONAL LOVE
Is
To know why and how
To rely on, learn from, and build upon:
★*the positive side of the Sleeping Giant in everyone,*
★*the Priceless Inner Treasure in everyone that is in no other,*
★*the life's most favorite Love Song in everyone that is in no other.*

Their own Words

Poet Hafiz asked the following question:

"Would You Think It Odd if Hafiz says?
I am in love with every church,
Every mosque,
And temple,
And every kind of shrine
Because I know it is there
That people say the different names
Of the same God."

Summary of the Chapter

Dear Spouses,
It is very difficult or even impossible
To have the will and skills and wisdom
You need
To love with true and long lasting *Love,*
To be loved with true and long lasting *Love,*
To enjoy and share true and long lasting *Peace*
With each other,
To enjoy and share true and long-lasting *Intimacy*
With each other
When one or both of you are in disconnection
With the ***infinite Self*** deep within you and all around you.
The frustrated will to meaning, to power,
The frustrated will to money,
The frustrated will to pleasure at its lowest level
Of one or both of you is due to your disconnection
With the *infinite Self* deep within you and all around both of you.
You both are created at the image and likeness
Of your *Creator;*

Your Creator is all-loving, all-knowing, all-powerful;
All loving, all-knowing, all-powerful
Is who you both are meant to be;
The larger the gap between whom you are divinely meant to be
And whom you happen to be in your day-to-day life,
The deeper the wound you may inflict on anyone close to you
Including the very innocent *Inner Child*
Deep within each and everyone you meet.

Dear spouses, are you willing to fight with all your might to know why and how to:

- ★ *love your own self with true and Unconditional Love?*
- ★ *love each other with true and Unconditional Love?*
- ★ *love all, including your hurtful friends and foes, with true and Unconditional Love?*

If *Yes* is your answer, you then need also to know why and how to see all men and all women of the whole world as the same important members of the same important family: the Human Family.

We human beings are the only creatures created *in the image* and *likeness of our Creator.*

We human beings are also the only creatures divinely, spiritually, and psychologically meant to be:

- ★ *all-loving,*
- ★ *all-knowing,*
- ★ *all-powerful.*

Some of the world great religious and spiritual traditions and collective wisdom tell us that:

- ★ *we each and all are created at God-image*
- ★ *we and all are created at God-likeness,*
- ★ *God is all-loving, all-knowing, all-powerful.*

Some of the world great *Spiritual* gurus tell us that we each and all are meant to enjoy and share *Oneness* with full *Self-awareness:*

- ★ *oneness with our own true, transcendent, infinite Self,*
- ★ *oneness with our loved ones and important others' true, transcendent, infinite Self,*
- ★ *oneness with everyone else's, including our enemies' true, transcendent, infinite Self.*

Some of the world's great poets and artists tell us that, at a certain level, the deepest or the highest level, we each and all are meant to be *One* with one another without losing our personal identity.

For instance, nineteenth-century French romantic poet,
Alfred de Lamartine said:

The distance between men
is neither the oceans nor the mountains.
The only distance between men
is their spirit.

Another nineteenth-century French poet,
Victor Hugo said:

When I am talking about myself,
I am talking about you,
Shame on you
if you think I am not you.

Some of the world depth psychologists and psychoanalysts
such as Carl G. Jung tell us that:

**socially, we all may be different from one social group to another,*
**historically, we all may be different from one*
historical group to the another,
**but psychologically, we each and all are One*
in our common Universal Heritage.

Dear spouses,
If you are to enjoy and share true and long lasting:
**love for each other,*
**peace with each other,*
**intimacy with each other*
You need to know why and how to:

★love your own self with true and long lasting Unconditional love,
★love each other with true and long lasting Unconditional love,
★love all with true and long-lasting Unconditional love.

When you know why and how to love each other with true and long-lasting *Unconditional love*, you will know how to reach and take advantage of your common *Universal Heritage.*

Our common universal heritage makes us all *One* with one another without losing our personal *Identity.*

Oneness with one another with full *Self-awareness* is what you need if you are to know why and how to:

- ★ *accept and respect and tolerate each other's natural difference,*
- ★ *be aware of each other's disabilities and yet still lean on their infinite possibilities,*
- ★ *forgive each other and heal and be whole even after divorce.*

As human beings, we are feeble, fallible, and vulnerable.

We each and all need to:

- ★ *be understood as who truly we are,*
- ★ *be accepted and respected as who truly we are meant to be,*
- ★ *enjoy and share our uniqueness, subjectivity, naivete, vulnerability...*

Unconditional love may involve but it encompasses, by far, our beauty, charm, elegance, deep knowledge, vast practical skills, power position, material possessions...

To love each other with *Unconditional love* is to inspire each other to know why and how to plunge into the deepest layers of our *Collective Unconscious.*

To love each other with *Unconditional love* is to inspire each other to know why and how to enjoy and share our common *universal heritage.*

Their own Story

An Example of the Amish Community's Unconditional Love

On October 2, 2006, CNN reported the following breaking news.

Carl Roberts, from Nickel Mine, Pennsylvania, went into an Amish School's room and shot, execution-style, five innocent school girls.

Then, he ended his own life with his own gun.

Roberts' tragic action shocked the world.

But, despite Roberts tragic action, the Amish Community reached out, hours later, to Roberts' wife and three children.

The Amish community showed no anger and no hatred against Roberts' family.

They rather set up a fund to support his wife and three kids.

Such extraordinary forgiveness does not happen very often.

Such extraordinary forgiveness comes only from those who know why and how to *Love* with true and long-lasting *UNCONDITIONAL LOVE.*

The Problem

Dear spouses, the twelfth major barrier to true *Love* and long lasting *Peace* and *Intimacy* every loving spouse needs to know is why and how to:

- *love their own self with true and long lasting Unconditional Love,*
- *love each other with true and long lasting Unconditional Love,*
- *love all with true and long-lasting Unconditional Love.*

The lack of *Unconditional Love* is due to:

- *the Soma/Spirit/Split,*
- *the parenting 3 massive mistakes,*
- *the dark and ugly side of the Personal Unconscious.*

Psychologically, we each and all are the same.

To some degree, we each and all are psychologically *One* with one another.

We each and all have access to the universal heritage or our *Collective Unconscious.*

Our access to the *Universal Source* is vital to the quality of our life and marriage.

But *the Soma/Spirit/Split, the parenting 3 massive mistakes, and the ugly, dark, and stubborn side of our Personal Unconscious* are 3 major barriers to the best there is within us and all around us all as a whole.

The Soma/Spirit/Split

Dear spouses, you live in two distinct yet intimately interconnected worlds.

You live, at the same time, in a material world and in a spiritual world.

You have both material needs and spiritual needs.

When you try to satisfy your material needs to the detriment of your spiritual needs, you undermine your built-in meaning-seeking and meaning-making machinery.

It's like *Hell* on earth to:

- ★ *live a meaningless life,*
- ★ *live a lifeless life,*
- ★ *die while seemingly alive.*

The negative consequences of the parenting 3 *Massive Mistake* may hunt you down for life by and through what Otto Rank and Carl G. Jung, call:

- ★ *the Fear of Life,*
- ★ *the Fear of Death,*
- ★ *the Empty Center.*

True and Unconditional Love is incompatible with any of the parenting 3 massive mistakes.

The dark, ugly, and stubborn side of your *Personal Unconscious* may often lead you to the ineffable and unbearable *Pain of Inner Emptiness* or what Viktor E. Frankl calls:

- ★ *the existential Vacuum,*
- ★ *the existential Frustration,*
- ★ *the frustrated will to meaning, to power, to money, to pleasure at its lowest level.*

The Solution

The *Solution* to the lack of *Unconditional Love* of one or both of you is to know why and how to inspire each other to:

- ★ *transcend the Soma/Spirit/Split,*
- ★ *overcome the negative consequences of the parenting 3 massive mistakes,*
- ★ *integrate the dark side of the Personal Unconscious into the Conscious attitudes.*

The heartfelt expression of your true and long lasting *Unconditional Love* for each other requires your:

- ★ *forgiveness, healing, wholeness...*
- ★ *inner purity, inner peace, inner autonomy...*
- ★ *true, transcendent, infinite Self...*

To love each other with true and long lasting *Unconditional Love* is to be open and receptive to:

- ★ *your own infinite Self,*
- ★ *each other's infinite Self,*
- ★ *everyone else's infinite Self.*

To love with *Unconditional Love* is to know why and how to:

- ★ *love all those who love you,*
- ★ *love all those who hate you,*
- ★ *forgive all those who hurt you.*

Dear spouses, one of your life greatest delight is to know why and how to:

- ★ *cease to be whom you used to be in order to be One with everyone else,*
- ★ *realize your own self by and through the realization of someone else,*
- ★ *pursue your ever-increasing inward but too often lonely journey from:*

    1. *cool calculation to your warm-hearted participation,*
    2. *vain glorious self-gratification to your compassionate association,*
    3. *your way as the only way to the middle as the ideal way to wisdom.*

Their own Story

In his book, *New Techniques of Inner Healing: Conversations with Contemporary Masters of Inner Healing (1992),* D. Scott Rogo reported the following religious experience.

The late Dr. Helen Schuman is well known as the New York A psychologist who channeled A Course In Miracle.

She experienced her first religious experience in an unlikely place.

She and her husband were riding a New York subway…

The scene was rather depressing, then suddenly a blinding light consumed her and she lost contact with her environment.

She saw herself within the light kneeling before somebody.

The light grew more and more intense and she felt an Unconditional Love emanating from it.

Soon she found herself loving everybody including the grubby people on the train.

She said:

"I saw a great light and waves upon waves of love
coming from it
and when I opened my eyes I loved everybody.
Then everything disappeared…
the feeling, everything."

In his own book, The Varieties of Religious Experiences, Physician, Philosopher, and Psychologist, Harvard professor Of psychology,
William James (1840-1910) is one of the first psychologists who gave scientific interest in these rather bizarre religious experiences.

Dr. Schuman turned immediately to her husband and described to him her...experience.

But he merely folded down the paper he was reading and said:
"Don't worry about it. It's a common mystical experience.
Don't give it another thought."

"The best and the most beautiful things in life,"
said, Helen Keller
"cannot be seen or...touched,
they must be felt by the heart."

CONCLUSION

Their own Words

Paulo Coello, the author of *The Alchemist,* said:

You will never ever reach your potential
if you don't open your heart.
You will never be able to escape from your heart.
So it's better to listen to what it has to say.

Dear spouses, the 12 *Vital* but too often missing *Life-Saving Signals* on your long and too often rocky and slippery road to true *Love* and long-lasting *Peace* and *Intimacy* are:

- ★ *the healthy and free and fully alive innocent Inner Child deep within both of you,*
- ★ *the true and long-lasting Fulfillment for both of you,*
- ★ *the true and long-lasting Inner Peace so vital to your Peace with each other,*
- ★ *Meaningfulness,*
- ★ *Mindfulness,*
- ★ *Foresightedness,*
- ★ *the more than Need-love,*
- ★ *the more than Gift-love,*
- ★ *the more than Mature love,*
- ★ *Healthy self-love,*
- ★ *Spiritual love,*
- ★ *Unconditional love.*

The 3 first major barriers on the long road to true *Love* and long lasting *Peace* and *Intimacy* with each other are:

- ★ *the wounded innocent Inner Child within one or both of you,*

- ★ *the deep and unfathomable Inner Void within one or both of you,*
- ★ *the unbearable Pain of Inner Emptiness within one or both of you.*

These 3 first deepest root causes of all *educational* issues at all levels are also the 3 deepest root causes of:

- ★ *the parenting 3 massive mistakes,*
- ★ *the dark and ugly and stubborn side of the Personal Unconscious,*
- ★ *the gap between the Persona-mask and the true and total Personality.*

Dear spouses, Excellence In Education is the rock-solid founding and building block of your *Oneness* with full *Self-awareness.* Your *Oneness* with full *Self-awareness, Oneness* with one another without losing your personal *Identity* is a true measure of your marriage's happiness.

Your *Oneness* with your own true *Self, Oneness* with each other's true *Self,* and *Oneness* with almost everyone else's true *Self* is a true measure of your true and long-lasting *Inner Peace.*

The emergence of each other's true, transcendent, infinite *Self* is vital to your ability to enjoy and share true and long-lasting:

- ★ *healthy self-love,*
- ★ *love fore each other,*
- ★ *peace and intimacy with each other.*

Your *Excellence In Education* has little or nothing to do with your:

- ★ *high academic achievement, deep knowledge, vast practical skills...*
- ★ *name, fame, celebrity, popularity, cheerful fans...*
- ★ *power position, material possessions, fancy cars, gorgeous houses...*

Your *Excellence In Education* has everything to do with your will, skills, and wisdom to:

- ★ *play in a common ground, your marriage ideal playground,*
- ★ *win the win-win marriage style, your marriage's ideal winning style,*
- ★ *stay in the middle, your marriage ideal pathway to stability and happiness.*

Their own Words

In his book, *Learning to Be Human*, psychotherapist,
Leston Havens is quoted having said that:

My mother remained married to my father
long after they were divorced.

My father, in fact, proposes a ceremony of divorce
congruent with
his concept of being human:

"Do you take this spouse as your former,
for better and for worse:
to be met at every graduation, marriage, and funeral?"
(re-adapted from *The Art of Marriage Maintenance*
by Sylvia R. Karasu, MD and T. Bryam Karasu, MD)

Dear spouses, according to Mother Teresa, it is not how much you give but how much love you put into the giving.

Mother Teresa's advice is to always have a cheerful smile and not only give your care but also give your heart as well.

To Mother Teresa, there is a terrible hunger for love. We all experience that hunger in our lives...the pain, the loneliness...and that we must have the courage to recognize it.

Their own Story

"A Little World of Happiness" from an Unlikely Teacher

Sigmund Freud is known as the father of psychoanalyse.

He has been one of the world's most brilliant minds
in human knowledge.

Freud calls Martha Bernays, his to-be fiance, "my dear sweet girl."

He met Marta at a family dinner in 1882.

Marta was twenty-one, Freud was twenty-six.

Freud was an ambitious researcher... at Bruche's physiological
collaborator in Vienna, Austria.

Freud and Marta's engagement lasted for four years.

The voluminous correspondence between Freud and Marta
during their long engagement period shows him
as a jealous and tyrannic and domineering lover.

He demanded unconditional love and utter veracity
about all Marta's relations and interactions with anyone
else including her loved ones and important others.

Freud wrote to Marta and said:
"...no matter how much they love you, I will not leave you
to anyone,
and no one deserves you; no one else's love compares to mine."

Marta met Freud's demands with both tack and spiritual resistance.
Marta's rights and need for relative independence were crucial to her.

Marta wrote to Freud and said:
"It would be a loss for us both...if I...love you as a dear little girl,
yet not as an equal, someone from whom I would have to hide
my thoughts and opinions---in short, the truth."

Marta's love for Freud and honesty and inalienable right and deep need for her own relative independence shifted Freud's views and tyrannical and domineering marriage's style.

That is how Marta, the unlikely teacher taught Freud,
one of the world's most brilliant minds in human knowledge.
Marta taught Freud how to get rid of his domineering love style.

That is how Freud and Marta build their "little world of happiness"
through their lifelong happy marriage.

Freud and Marta were finally wed in late September 1886
and their marriage lasted the length of their lives over fifty years.

Dear spouses, anytime you wonder why and how to enjoy and share true *Love* and long-lasting *Peace* and *Intimacy* with each other, remember King Solomon and the Queen of Sheba's love story.

You may have heard about King Solomon.
He was one of the most powerful biblical King.
He was also the richest man who ever lived.
He had hundreds of wives and concubines

But Solomon, the powerful and wealthy King,
knelt down before one woman.
He knelt down with a smile on his face all his way down.
That woman was the Queen of Sheba.

What was so special about the Queen of Sheba?
What did she have more than Solomon's
Other wives (s) and concubines?

The answer seems simple.

The Queen of Sheba had an authentic *Self.*
She loved her own self with *healthy self-love.*
She did not love Solomon solely because he was
a powerful King.
She did not love Solomon merely because he was
the richest man who ever lived.
She loved Solomon as an equal.
That was it.
That was enough to touch the King's heart.
That was enough to conquer the King's heart.
That was enough to make all the difference.

REFERENCES

Alice Gray: *Stories For The Heart: Over 100 Stories To Encourage Your Soul.* Quester Publishing, Inc., Sisters, Oregon, 1996.

Andrea J. Moses: *Creating Happiness By Breaking Free From Your Past.* Powerbase Communication, Toronto, Ontario, Canada, 1994.

Barbara De Angelis: *Secrets About Life Every Woman Should Know: Ten Principles For Total Emotional and Spiritual Fulfillment.* Hyperion, New York, NY, 1999.

Brian Culhane: *The Treasure Chest: Memorable Words Of Wisdom And Inspiration.* Harpers Collins Publisher, New York, NY, 1995.

Charlotte D. Kasl: *Find Joy: 101 Ways To Free Your Spirit And Dance With Life.* Harpers Collins Publisher, New York, NY, 1994.

D. Scott Rogo: *New Techniques of Inner Healing: Conversations With Contemporary Masters of Alternative Healing.* Paragon House, New York, 1992.

Eckhart Tolle: *The Power of Now: A Guide to Spiritual Enlightenment.* Namaste Publishing, Vancouver, Canada, 1999.

Ellen J. Langer: *The Power of Mindful Learning.* A Merloyd Lawrence Book, Massachusetts, 1989.

Ellen J. Langer: *The Power of Mindful Learning.* A Merloyd Lawrence Book, Massachusetts, 1997.

Ferrari, M., & Sternberg R.: *Self-Awareness: Its Nature and Development.* The Guilford Press, New York,1998.

Gary Chapman: *Love As A Way Of Life: Seven Keys To Transforming Every Aspect Of Your Life.* Doubleday, New York, 2008.

Gibran Kahlil: *The Prophet.* Alfred Knop, New York, 1923.

Hal Urban: *Choices That Change Lives:15 Ways To Find More Purpose*, Meaning, and Joy. Fireside/Simon & Schuster, Inc.,2006.

James William: *The Varieties Of Religious Experiences.*The Modern Library, New York, 1929.

Jeremiah Abram: *Reclaiming The Inner Child.* Jeremy P. Tarcher, Inc., Los Angeles, 1990.

John Edward: *Infinite Quest: Develop Your Psychic Intuition To Take Charge of Your Own Life.* Sterling Publishing, New York, 2010.

John-Roger: *Spiritual Warrior: The Art of Spiritual Living.* Madewell Press, Los Angeles. CA, 2008.

John Schuster: *Answering Your Calling: A Guide For Living Your Deep Purpose.* Berrett Koehler Publishers, Inc., San Francisco, 2003.

Jonathan Starr: *An Inner Treasure: An Introduction To The World's Sacred and Mystical Writings.* Jeremy P. Tarcher/Putman, New York, NY, 1999.

Joseph A. Matter: *Love, Altruism and The World Crisis: Challenge of Pitirim Sorokin.* Little Adam & CO, Totowa, New Jersey.

Joseph Campbell: *Spiritual Disciplines: Papers From The Eranos Yearbooks.* Volume 4, Princeton University Press, New Jersey, 1960.

Johnston William: *The Inner Eye Of Love: Mysticism And Religion.* Fordham University Press, New York, 1997,

Leonard George: *The Silent Pulse: A Search For the Perfect Rhythm That Exists in Each One Of Us.* Gibbs Smith Publisher, Utah, 2006.

Lewis M. Andrew: *To Thine Own Self Be True: The Relationship Between Spiritual Values and Emotional Health.* Doubleday Dell Publishing, Group, Inc., New York 1987,1989.

Malick Kouyate: *The Power Of The Powerful.* Outskirts Press, 2009.

Malick Kouyate: *Love: The Young Adults' Road To A More Meaningful Life.* Booksurge, 2009.

Malick Kouyate: *How To Educate All For Excellence: Excellent Learners' 7 Deepest Educational Needs.* Trafford Publishing, 2013.

Malick Kouyate: Dear Parents Listen To Your Teens Unheard Cry

Murray Stein: *Jung's Map Of The Soul: An Introduction.* Open Court Publishing Company Peru, IL,1998.

Os Guinness: *Long Journey HOME: A Guide To Your Search For The Meaning Of Your Life.* WaterBrook Press & Doubleday, 2001.

Osche R.: *Before The Gate Of Excellence: The Determinant Of Creative Genius.* Cambridge University Press,1990.

Sidney M. Jourard: *The Transparent Self.* Van Nostrand Reinhold Company, New York, NY, 1971.

Steven K. Scoot: *The Richest Man Who Ever Lived: King Solomon's Secrets To Success, Wealth and Happiness.* Doubleday Publishing, 2006.

Scott D.. Roco: *New Techniques Of Inner Healing: Conversations With Contemporary Masters Of Alternative Healing.* Paragon House, New York. 2008.

Ralph Waldo Emerson: *Essays and Lectures*: University of Cambridge Press. UK,1983.

Ralph Waldo Trine: *In Tune With The Infinite.* Jeremy P. Tarcher/Penguin, New York, 2008.

Rumi Jalal Uddin: *The Soul Of Rumi.* Translated by C. Barks. Harper Collins, San Franscico, 2002.

Wayne W. Dyer: *Change Your Thoughts: Change Your Life.* Hay House, Inc., 2007.

Wayne Teasdale: *The Mystic Heart: Discovering A Universal Spirituality In The World Religions.* New World Library, Novato, CA, 1999.

Printed in the United States
by Baker & Taylor Publisher Services